NEUTRALIZATION
AND
WORLD POLITICS

PUBLISHED FOR
THE CENTER OF INTERNATIONAL STUDIES
PRINCETON UNIVERSITY
A LIST OF OTHER CENTER PUBLICATIONS
APPEARS AT THE BACK OF THIS BOOK

Neutralization

AND WORLD POLITICS

CYRIL E. BLACK

RICHARD A. FALK

KLAUS KNORR

ORAN R. YOUNG

PRINCETON, NEW JERSEY

PRINCETON UNIVERSITY PRESS

1968

PREFACE

THE neutralization of Switzerland, Belgium, and Luxembourg in the nineteenth century reminds us that a status of permanent neutrality was once a significant means of managing power in the international system. After a considerable lapse interest in neutralization has been revived, partly stimulated by the settlements negotiated for Austria in 1955 and Laos in 1962 and partly encouraged by public figures such as Senator Fulbright, President de Gaulle, Governor Romney, and George Kennan, who have proposed neutralization as a political compromise that might bring the Vietnam war to an end.

At the invitation of the Senate Foreign Relations Committee we undertook in the spring of 1966 to do a short study of the applicability of neutralization to the problems of conflict in Southeast Asia, especially Vietnam.[1] As a result of that experience, we became convinced that the idea of neutralization deserved a fuller treatment than it has heretofore received in the contemporary literature of international relations. This volume tries to satisfy this need in a preliminary way, not by purporting to be a definitive work, but by examining the principal issues in sufficient detail to promote an understanding of the appeals and hazards of neutralization as a concept relevant to the avoidance or settlement of an international conflict.

Neutralization is a concept of limited applicability. As we try to make clear, especially in Chapter IV, principal sovereign states are not suitable candidates for neutralization. In fact, neutralization seems potentially attractive only for relatively minor states that, by reason of stra-

[1] "Neutralization in Southeast Asia: Problems and Prospects," A Study Prepared at the Request of the Committee on Foreign Relations, United States Senate (Washington, D.C., October 10, 1966).

tegic position or symbolic political value, have become or threaten to become the focal points of contests for control or dominant influence between principal regional or global rivals. There are a number of situations around the world in which the struggle for control of minor states is dangerous and destructive and for which neutralization may offer a way out in the form of diplomatic compromise.

Neutralization, in effect, is a formal status of permanent neutrality. The specific attributes of the status reflect the outcome of international negotiations. There is no single, clearly specifiable concept of neutralization but rather a variety of potential forms available to express the particular convergence of negotiating interests that results in a neutralization agreement. Neutralization is not normally thought of as an imposed status, since it reflects an agreement between the government of the neutralized state and the governments of external rival states variously concerned about its welfare and autonomy. These external states may function as guarantors of neutralization, undertaking to respect the status and perhaps even accepting a duty to act to uphold the agreement if it is jeopardized.

In the main, then, neutralization should be understood as a flexible instrumentality of statecraft. Its role is limited to the search for ways to remove minor states from arenas of destructive regional and global competition. In an era of stalemate and standoff, accented by the hazards of nuclear confrontation, there is room in diplomacy for techniques designed to transform military stalemates into political stalemates. Neutralization offers the possibility for such a transformation in some circumstances, especially those wherein a minor state is the scene of domestic strife and competitive intervention. The ex-colonial world provides a number of national settings in which are exhibited these vulnerabilities to sustained violent, but inconclusive, competition for dominant control.

The difficulty of agreeing on the terms of neutralization should not be underestimated, nor should the problems of maintaining the status once agreed upon. The viability of neutralization is acutely dependent on the existence and reasonable continuity of convergent (though not necessarily common) interests among the concerned governments. Nevertheless, despite all the problems of negotiating and maintaining neutralization, it may yet be less problematic in a given context than any alternative. Neutralization, if diligently considered, may surprisingly turn out to be negotiable, if only because it qualifies as the least flawed diplomatic alternative for a state in question.

We hope this volume will encourage the diligent consideration of neutralization in certain situations of conflict. In particular, we hope the possibility of neutralization will enter seriously into the debate about the shape and substance of a Vietnam settlement. Beyond the specific challenge of Southeast Asia, we hope neutralization might be given its due in the repertoire of contemporary statecraft as one among several instrumentalities for the management of power.

The authors would like to take this opportunity to thank William J. McClung and Sanford G. Thatcher, of the Princeton University Press, for their encouragement and careful editorial assistance. They also wish to thank Stephen Fuzesi, Jr., a Princeton undergraduate, for making available to them his interesting analysis of the negotiations leading to the neutralization agreement on Laos in 1962.

Cyril E. Black
Richard A. Falk
Klaus Knorr
Oran R. Young

CONTENTS

INTRODUCTION

DEFINITION AND CHARACTERISTICS

A conventional definition of neutralization typically reads as follows: *A neutralized state is one whose political independence and territorial integrity are guaranteed permanently by a collective agreement of great powers, subject to the conditions that the neutralized state will not take up arms against another state, except to defend itself, and will not assume treaty obligations which may compromise its neutralized status.* The status of neutralization is often referred to as *permanent* neutrality to signify that it is valid in times of peace as well as war. Neutralization has assumed in the past, and may take in the future, many diverse forms which this narrow definition does not fit. A definition covering all cases, one that will necessarily be abstract, may be put in the following terms: *Neutralization is a special international status designed to restrict the intrusion of specified state actions in a specified area.* Only as the range of variations is noted will the concept of neutralization, so defined, acquire more content.

Three kinds of areas are subject to neutralization: first, inhabited territories with internationally recognized governments, such as Switzerland, Austria, and Laos; second, inhabited territories without internationally recognized governments, of which the Gaza Strip and Kashmir are examples; and, third, uninhabited regions, like Antarctica, rivers and waterways, and outer space. Although all three kinds of areas can be neutralized in the sense that neutralization regulates the actions of outside states toward them, uninhabited areas and inhabited areas lacking recognized governments constitute special cases. For only inhabited territories with effective and recognized governments can assume a reciprocal regulation of actions vis-à-vis outside states; and such complementary obligations are, as we shall see, an important part of the classical instances of neutralization.

The regulation of state behavior toward an uninhabited neutralized area may take such forms as prohibiting its use for military purposes—the establishment of military bases, for instance—or interdicting the acquisition of national sovereignty over all or portions of the area concerned. State behavior toward an inhabited neutralized territory may be regulated in terms of either or both of two obligations—namely, not to attack militarily and not to interfere with the internal affairs of the neutralized territory. However, as already stated, where the area involved is an inhabited territory with a recognized government, these obligations are balanced by reciprocal obligations on the part of the neutralized state. These restrictions may include undertakings not to use military force except in self-defense, not to permit other states to use its territory for military purposes or to interfere with its domestic affairs, not to enter alliances or other international agreements compromising its neutralized status, and not to intervene in the domestic affairs of other states.

Permanent neutrality is a special international status which normally is brought about by international agreement between the state-to-be-neutralized and either a group of great powers (like that which guaranteed the neutralization of Switzerland in 1815) or a group of small as well as great powers (like that which negotiated the settlement in Laos in 1962). There is no legal reason, of course, why a small state should not be neutralized by agreement with neighboring small powers. A state may also neutralize itself by means of a unilateral declaration, an act which acquires international status as soon as it is recognized by other states.[1] Thus, the self-neutralization of Austria in 1955, promoted by the Soviet government, was recognized by the Soviet Union, the United States, the United Kingdom, France, and the other countries with which it had diplomatic relations. This form of permanent neutrality, recognized by other states, is less clearly defined than the status resulting from an international neutralization treaty, but its effectiveness depends more on political realities than on formal commitments.

An international neutralization agreement specifies a set of reciprocal obligations of the kind mentioned above and usually also makes varying provisions for its enforcement. The normal enforcement provision is a guarantee by the other signatory powers to assist the neutralized state in the maintenance of its status and particularly to come to its aid when this status has been violated by deliberate aggression. In principle, such a guarantee can impose three kinds of responsibility on the guarantor states: first, collective; second, individual; and third, both collective and individual. The last kind is called a joint-and-several guarantee. A neutralization agreement may also create instruments for assisting in its enforcement—for example, machinery for verifying the observation of treaty provisions. Thus, the 1962 agreement on the neutralization of Laos set up a control commission for this very purpose.

Although neutralization agreements often stipulate that the neutral status be permanent, there is no reason

---

[1] Sweden, though it shuns alliances and pursues a policy of neutrality in the event of war, does not enjoy such a legally recognized status. The same holds true of Cambodia. These states are, of course, free to change their policy at any time.

why neutralization cannot be limited to varying specified periods of time.

Demilitarization, which is sometimes confused with neutralization, is clearly a different measure, although it too may involve international guarantees. According to the historical record, neutralized states have rarely been demilitarized. The demilitarization of the Rhineland (1919–1935) did not neutralize that part of Germany from a political standpoint. Demilitarization simply deprives the inhabitants of an area of organized military force; it does not—as neutralization, if it fulfills its basic function, does—control the actions of *other* states toward the area involved or neutralize the area politically. However, demilitarization of a state or city, or part of a state, may be associated with neutralization.

Neutralism and neutralization are quite different phenomena. Countries such as Yugoslavia, the United Arab Republic, India, and Burma, which have from time to time defined for themselves a neutralist posture, meant to do no more than dissociate themselves, for various reasons, from the worldwide struggle for influence between the Communist powers, on the one hand, and the United States and its allies, on the other.[2] Indeed, most neutralist states vigorously condemned this struggle. But they wanted to be nonaligned only with reference to this East-West antagonism. They did not want to become neutralized, even in the sense of self-neutralization, and accept the obligations that neutralization imposes.

Neutralization also differs from *neutrality.* Neutrality is similar to neutralism in that it describes the posture of a state vis-à-vis a conflict—usually a military conflict—

[2] Cf. Peter Lyon, *Neutralism* (Leicester 1963), especially Chaps. I and VII.

between other states. It is a policy of nonparticipation in ongoing wars. It is not, like neutralization, concerned with preventing, moderating, or terminating interstate coercion. Unlike neutralism, however, neutrality is a legal status as well as a diplomatic or political posture. It may be said, of course, that neutralization means *permanent* neutrality, rather than neutrality only in time of formal hostilities.

FUNCTIONS OF NEUTRALIZATION

The primary functions of neutralization are examined in Chapter I. It may be useful to summarize these functions as they relate to different kinds of states according to their roles in neutralization. From the viewpoint of all states involved, neutralization may serve to stabilize an unstable international situation or prevent the status quo in an area from becoming seriously disturbed, if not upset, by means of coercion. The function of neutralization is, then, one of bolstering international order, of regulating interstate coercion, of leaving the settlement of international disputes concerned with the neutralized state to the play of accepted international norms and institutions and to diplomacy. From the viewpoint of the neutralized state, the effect of neutralization is to support its military security and its political and territorial integrity. From the viewpoint of the guarantor states with a strong and competitive interest in the status of the neutralized area, neutralization may restrain or stop them from engaging in military actions which are costly in various ways, above all, those which threaten to escalate into a major and dangerous war between themselves. Also from the viewpoint of the great powers, or from that of neighboring states, neutralization may help prevent the international balance of power from becoming upset to their disadvantage.

The functions of neutralization lend themselves to historical study. This is carried out in Chapters II and III. The present book is not, however, primarily historical. Its focus is on the utility of neutralization in the contemporary world, and the historical chapters are therefore selective, examining precedents that seem to have contemporary relevance and ignoring or slighting those that do not.

PROBLEMS

As Chapter I points out, neutralization is only one technique of statecraft for regulating interstate coercion and supporting or restoring international order. The prerequisites for its utility—that is, for its establishment and maintenance—are largely peculiar to its characteristics. As a means of preserving international peace and tranquility, or of terminating or moderating international conflicts, it is, therefore, more practicable in some situations than in others and will be quite irrelevant in still others. These problems are analyzed in Chapter IV.

One peculiarity of neutralization is simply that, except in the case of self-neutralization, it must be negotiated between governments at least some of which may be competing for influence in the area under consideration. This is always so when neutralization is a meliorative rather than a preventive measure, when it is a question of terminating and dampening interstate coercion rather than one of avoiding such entanglement. Neutralization can come about only if the interests of the states concerned are sufficiently convergent and only if the interests engaged are not just those directly at stake in connection with the area to be neutralized. For the great powers, these interests derive also from the overall global relationships between them and from their governments' expectations of how the acceptance of neutralization may be interpreted by other governments as an index of their states' position and power. The complexities of negotiation are discussed in Chapter V.

Neutralization raises problems of maintenance and enforcement. If the neutralized state has an efficient government and a politically cohesive population, it may be vulnerable to armed attack by stronger states, but it is invulnerable to indirect forms of coercive intervention. Violation of its neutral status by direct military attack is highly visible, as was the invasion of Belgium in 1914. The likelihood of such violations hinges on the reprisals which the violating state expects to incur. When a neutralized state is vulnerable to other forms of interventionist coercion, and perhaps already subject to such intervention, redoubtable problems of control and enforcement are apt to arise. Their nature and severity depend upon the character of the neutralized area, upon the access and resources available to actual or potential intervening powers, and upon the political stakes which led, or might lead, to unilateral or competitive intervention in its internal affairs. In order to cope with the difficulties of preventing, terminating, or at least moderating such intervention, neutralization agreements may specify appropriate organs to undertake supervision and control. This group of problems is studied in Chapter VI.

Finally, neutralization must be considered in relation to the peacekeeping functions of the United Nations and regional organizations. If the United Nations were fully effective in enforcing its Charter and if it defined peacekeeping more clearly with reference to what has been called in UN circles "indirect aggression" as well as in regard to direct aggression, the need for neutralization would disappear. Since these shortcomings have not yet been overcome, neutralization can be regarded as an instrument of peacekeeping complementary to the activities of the UN, supporting its mission. It is certainly conceivable that the UN, in turn, might support measures of neutralization in connection, for example, with negotiation, supervision, control, and enforcement. On the other hand, there is the question of whether or not the rules of conduct imposed upon the neutralized state are compatible with the responsibilities of UN membership implied in the collective-security provisions of the Charter. Membership in regional security organizations may pose similar questions. These matters are explored in Chapters III and VII.

NEUTRALIZATION
AND
WORLD POLITICS

CHAPTER I

NEUTRALIZATION AND THE MANAGEMENT OF POWER IN THE INTERNATIONAL SYSTEM

IN 1815 the Congress of Vienna agreed on the neutralization of Switzerland as part of a general settlement after the bloody upheavals that had been touched off by the French Revolution and Napoleon's drive for a continental empire. The powers assembled at Vienna were concerned with stabilizing the European system, which to their way of thinking at the time was the core of the international system. The neutralization of Switzerland, though only a small part of the total settlement, was a conscious act of preventive diplomacy. It was meant to thwart any upset of the new balance of power, particularly an upset engineered by any power or coalition of powers conquering or bringing into a military alliance this small country, which had common boundaries with France, Austria, and several German and Italian states and which controlled vital lines of communication.

In 1955 France, Britain, and the United States acquiesced in the neutralization of Austria at the behest of the Soviet Union, paving the way to a termination of this country's postwar occupation and the restoration of its sovereign independence. This act was not part of a general postwar settlement. Indeed, the middle 1950s witnessed the solidification of two antagonistic alliance systems, which accentuated the division of the European continent. Nevertheless, a small country, located on the dividing line and occupying a crossroads of strategic significance, was by common accord removed from contention between the two blocs. This act of statesmanship not only liberated a nation from foreign domination but also excised a source of dangerous instability in a particular geographic area.

In 1962 a large number of states, including the United States, the Soviet Union, and the People's Republic of China, agreed to neutralize strife-torn Laos, in which three local factions, backed by outside powers, were involved in protracted civil war. Again, this act was not part of a general or regional settlement. Nor was its purpose to prevent international conflict over a weak country. The aim, rather, was to terminate if possible, or at least to moderate, a conflict which, if left wholly unregulated, would remain a source of highly disturbing instability in the area and, therefore, have the potential to expand into a more dangerous conflagration.

These three examples, to which more could be added, remind us that at various times in the past the great powers, and smaller states as well, have regarded neutralization as a useful instrument for bolstering international stability, or dampening international instability, to their mutual advantage.

When a sovereign state is neutralized by international agreement, that state is obligated to refrain from using its military forces for any purpose but self-defense and the maintenance of internal order, from entering into military alliances with other states, and from allowing other states to use its territory for military purposes. The other parties to a neutralization treaty are always under the obligation to respect the status and integrity of the neutralized state; often they are also required by the agreement to come to the aid of the neutralized state in the event that its status and integrity are violated by another power. They then become guarantors of the neutralization act.

The primary aim of neutralization is to insulate the neutralized state or area against certain forms of international contention. The neutralized state, which, if it is a member of the United Nations, has already renounced the legal freedom to engage in military aggression against other states, gives up the additional freedom to enter upon military undertakings with other powers; in exchange, it gains in security. The guarantor states commit themselves not to exercise certain kinds of coercive acts against the neutralized state, and perhaps to come to its aid if its status is violated; in exchange, they gain from the lessened vulnerability of the neutralized state to the coercive power of their competitors and from a diminished risk of a dangerous military confrontation with these rivals.

In the event that a state is neutralized when already subject to a conflict involving competitive intervention by outside powers, neutralization serves the purpose of *conflict termination,* or at least of *conflict moderation.* If this status is conferred on a state not currently in such difficulties, neutralization serves the purpose of *conflict avoidance.* In either case, neutralization is a technique for international conflict management, for restraining, and hence regulating to a degree, the exercise of power in part of the international system.

As it did at the time of the Congress of Vienna, neutralization is apt to find use as a technique of conflict avoidance, that is, as a precautionary measure. This function of neutralization comes into play when the main powers share a strong interest in averting a relapse into costly forms of strife, when the balance of shared interests favors cooperation rather than competitive behavior. It is the prevention of undue damage and risk which then causes the powers to acquiesce in the neutralization of an area that is potentially an attractive bone of contention. Contrariwise, when competitive interests tend to dominate cooperative interests and when the outbreak of conflicts therefore has a high incidence, neutralization may appeal as an instrument for terminating, or at least moderating, a particularly costly and dangerous conflict; that is, it may commend itself as a meliorative measure. This function will tend to be emphasized when neutralization may serve as a means for transforming a stalemate which is unstable, costly, and dangerous into one which is more stable, less costly, and less dangerous. It is then the reduction of military losses and risk which forms the necessary basis for agreement.

These possibilities raise the question of whether this tool for restraining the use of international coercive power could not be made to serve the same end in the contemporary world, in which areas of acute and potential instability abound and in which some of the great and medium powers nevertheless show signs of recognizing a common interest in moderating unstable situations.

The two superpowers especially, as they continue to pursue antagonistic goals, tend to become involved in these situations, sometimes with considerable reluctance, particularly when their aims are essentially defensive rather than acquisitive. Involvement stems from the desire to deny the rival power any appreciable gains in international influence or to reduce its influence and increase one's own. Thus, the United States and the Soviet Union act as rivals in the unstable situations in the Middle East. Other powers, too, may become part of the network of entanglements. In Southeast Asia, and also in the South of Asia, competitive contention is pitting the United States against China and China against the Soviet Union, as well as the Soviet Union against the United States.

Strong as their competitive urges apparently are, the governments of these countries have shown marked reluctance to press their pursuit of conflict to a point at which it might escalate uncontrollably into a hazardous military encounter. To this extent, at least, they share an incentive to cooperate. And to this extent neutralization may invite attention both for terminating or dampening conflicts which have reached an alarming level of danger or impose other costs of unwelcome, if not unacceptable, magnitude and as a means of avoiding future involvement in conflicts of this kind in certain areas.

In cases of conflict in third areas, a basis for agreeing on neutralization would have to be provided either, as already remarked, by the shared desire to render a stalemate more stable and less dangerous or by a mutual interest in supplying a face-saving retreat from a situation that has become excessively burdensome to one of the contenders. In either case, interests might be sufficiently convergent to make this form of conflict moderation or conflict termination attractive.

There are also some characteristics of the contemporary world which would seem to make an interest in neutralization as an instrument of conflict avoidance something less than a far-fetched idea. These are characteristics which make the propensity for exercising international coercion very high at the present time. Two forms of coercion must be distinguished in this respect. One is the classical form of military aggression, that is to say, the armed attack, or threat thereof, by one state against another. Although neutralization has been found useful in the past for minimizing this type of coercion, it is not a kind particularly favored in the contemporary world. There are various restraints, including those embedded in the United Nations Charter, which militate against its practice, especially by great and middle powers against weaker states. Much more frequently undertaken is coercive intervention in the internal affairs of states by means of fomenting, or meddling in, civil strife, as well as engaging in other practices which are subversive of the constituted authority in weaker states.

Several conditions combine to generate the high frequency of this type of international coercion at the present time. First, there is a great disparity of strength between states in terms of administrative, economic, and technological, as well as military, resources. Second, a large number of new states are weak not only militarily but politically; they lack efficient government and political unity. Engaged in the process of political, economic, and social change, they necessarily develop instabilities as traditional modes of life become eroded while new modes, better adapted to the aspirations of elites and masses, have not yet become consolidated. These instabilities, in turn, have a strong tendency to produce political division and civil strife. Third, since the elites of many of these underdeveloped societies are intent on rapid development at a rate appreciably faster than indigenous capabilities permit, they are eager to receive aid from wealthier states; and the resulting dependence of the weaker states affords avenues for interventionist policies on the part of the stronger countries.

If these three conditions offer ample opportunities for coercive intervention, a further condition supplies the great powers with strong motives for seizing these opportunities. The Soviet Union and the People's Republic of

China—though competing against each other, especially in Asia—are avowedly bent on revising the present international status quo. Both aspire to the ultimate replacement of the English-speaking and the West European states, and the states associated with them, by states organized in their own ideological image. More immediately, both are determined to increase their own influence in world affairs and reduce that of the United States, which they regard as the citadel "of capitalist imperialism." It is equally obvious that the United States opposes these revisionist drives and is firmly resolved to resist them.

These are the conditions that beget competitive coercive intervention by strong states in the internal affairs of weaker countries and that tend to make such intervention both extensive and intensive. Because interventions of this sort may turn out to be costly in lives and treasure to the intervenor as well as to the victim, however, and because they contain the makings of dangerous military clashes between the great powers involved, international arrangements which terminate or moderate these interventions, or prevent them altogether, and which would thus regulate the use of coercion in the international system might prove highly useful.

Beyond doubt, most of the smaller and weaker states would benefit from such regulation. Not only would they stand to suffer in the event that the big powers clashed militarily; they are also the actual or potential victims of competitive international coercion, for they furnish the theater of operations for the moves and countermoves of great power rivals. They clearly should be interested in any arrangements that would raise the threshold against foreign intrusion and would thereby lower the prerequisites for their integrity and very survival.

9

The critical question is, of course, whether the mixed interests of the great powers converge sufficiently to permit such arrangements to be worked out. At first sight, the question seems especially apposite with reference to neutralization, which may be thought of as freezing the international status quo. Given their strong determination to revise the status quo, why should the leading Communist powers accept neutralization, except perhaps as a temporary tactical move in a situation in which the balance of strength happens to work against them? The fact of the matter is, however, that neutralization need not freeze the international status quo. For one thing, as already observed, neutralization could serve occasionally as a face-saving measure by means of which an intervening power could withdraw from an entanglement that had turned unacceptably costly and hazardous. In this case, a change in the status quo would only be masked temporarily. More important, neutralization would help preserve the freedom of societies to choose their own form of government and course of development. If the governments and elites of the great Communist powers really have confidence in the thrust of the historical forces which they expect to doom capitalist regimes, then they should be willing to rely on these forces and abet them only by means not prohibited by new rules of the game. Similarly, if the United States really believes in national self-determination, it should be prepared to accept the consequences of any foreign revolutions resulting from the play of indigenous political forces—even if their complexion is anathema to its ideological desiderata. Neutralization does not, in these important respects, freeze the status quo. Its only effect is to inhibit coercive intervention from outside. The strong powers would simply exchange the freedom to intervene for a condition which would minimize the need to counterintervene in defense of their interests and which would save them the appreciable costs and risks of intervention. This arrangement would be a bargain in many instances.

Notwithstanding the neutralization of Austria and Laos, neutralization is hardly a fashionable notion among contemporary statesmen. In view of its history, a disposition to consider it as a possible method for solving local problems of international order is widely diffused in Europe. It is also clear that, in the mid-1950s, Soviet leaders were strongly attracted by the idea of neutralization for application in Asia as well as in Central Europe. In line with the new policy of "peaceful coexistence," they explored the practicability of creating "gray zones" of neutral states between the Western and Soviet alliance systems. But this attempt failed to win the support of the United States. In fact, there is no evidence that American policymakers have thus far been attracted by the concept. The foregoing analysis suggests, however, that it merits study by responsible statesmen and that there are factors at work in the contemporary world which may induce them to give it their attention.

It would be wildly unrealistic, of course, to regard neutralization as a panacea for managing power in the present international system. Perhaps the caution evoked by the fear of uncontrollable military escalation, the heavy costs of intervention incurred in particular instances in the past, the considerable probability of failure which past experience suggests, accompanied by a gradual rise in the effectiveness of internationally sanctioned norms of state behavior, will cause the governments of the great powers to restrain themselves and to coordinate this restraint to some degree by means of tacit understandings. And, after all, there are other instruments for managing power in the international system. Specific techniques of statecraft which have served to some extent to regulate interstate coercion in the past do still exist. One is the balance of power, another the establishment of alliances and acknowledged spheres of influence. Finally, though so far largely a failure when implementation has been tried, there is the concept of collective security, contained especially in the United Nations Charter, but also embodied in regional organizations. All these techniques for curbing the exercise of international coercion may contribute to bring order to the world, or to particular geographic areas, in the future as they have often done in the past. All that can be claimed is that the concept of neutralization deserves to be accepted as one instrument in the tool kit of statesmen and considered seriously when conditions favor its employment.

There is, indeed, no question that neutralization has drawbacks and defects like all techniques available for preserving, bolstering, or restoring international order. The relatively sparing use made of neutralization is no doubt a reflection of its disadvantages. Whatever may be the benefits that accrue to a neutralized state, neutralization also places severe limits on its freedom of action. It must renounce the use of force, except in self-defense, and the practice of indirect aggression against other states. If it has allies, it must break its military ties with them. In the event of civil war, its government must refrain from inviting a foreign power to suppress domestic rebels. As Soviet opposition to Austria's desire to join the European Economic Community and Swiss absence from the United Nations show, it may be prevented from joining regional or global organizations if membership

12

might compromise its status. In short, the neutralized state is variously restricted in its foreign policy. According to the historical record, no great or middle power has ever been a candidate for neutralization, and it may be taken for granted that no state aspiring to such rank will find neutralization an attractive status. It may even be that some nations find it a degrading status, though the Swiss obviously do not.[1] All these disadvantages, and perhaps other obligations spelled out in a neutralization treaty, must be accepted even though neutralization may prove ineffective.

Guarantor states, in turn, must forego coercive policies against a neutralized state, unless they are prepared to tolerate the consequences of violating neutralization. Guarantor states, for instance, must refrain from supporting domestic revolutionaries against the government of the neutralized state or from supporting that government against domestic rebels by means proscribed in the neutralization agreement. Furthermore, the guaranteeing states undertake the obligation—involving potential costs and risks—to come to the aid of the neutralized state in the event that its status is violated. This form of advance commitment is a particularly serious obligation, much more onerous than the vaguer commitment assumed under the United Nations Charter, though perhaps no more burdensome than commitments involved in military alliances.

The attractiveness of neutralization hinges on government forecasts regarding the relative effectiveness of any particular scheme of neutralization. Any anxiety about

[1] The Swiss are proud of their neutralized status in large part because the guarantee of the guarantor states has lost most of its meaning and their status is seen to rest principally on Swiss military preparedness.

the element of uncertainty in such estimates may be tempered by the enforcement provisions laid down in the neutralization agreement. Especially if the agreement contains a joint-and-several guarantee, and also, of course, if the neutralization scheme collapses, each state recovers its freedom of action upon violation of the agreement. A guaranteeing power may thus proceed to counterintervention; and, because neutralization had been violated by an aggressor, it might do so on internationally acceptable grounds. This prospect is not, however, necessarily or completely reassuring. As a result of one-sided intervention, the violating state may have gained in the violated state an advantageous position from which it is difficult to dislodge it. Or the guaranteeing state, upon recovering its freedom of action, may find its capabilities for counterintervention at least temporarily reduced compared with the situation that prevailed prior to the act of neutralization. This might be the case especially if the guaranteeing state in question were geographically far removed from the state whose neutralization had been violated. As noted below, furthermore, counterintervention is an initiative which, unless properly authorized, runs counter to obligations assumed under the United Nations Charter.

A final and major disadvantage of neutralization is simply that, except in the case of self-neutralization, it must be negotiated between governments at least some of which are competing for influence in the area concerned. The negotiation of a neutralization agreement, particularly in a politically unstable area, is apt to encounter difficulties peculiar to the problems of neutralization. As already mentioned, from the viewpoint of great power involvement, neutralization constitutes the acceptance of a stalemate or offers the means for a face-saving exit. On top of these problems that are peculiar to the act of neutralization, the overall relationship between the great powers is likely to influence the bargaining positions of their governments, as will their expectations that the bargaining outcome may be widely interpreted as an index of the relative power enjoyed by their countries.

Whether, regarding any possible area for neutralization, net advantages are perceived by the governments of the main states involved, so that neutralization becomes negotiable, is an empirical question. It is a question capable of settlement only with reference to the particular circumstances of particular situations. The answer can be ascertained only through the process of negotiation. But negotiation will not, of course, be contemplated, let alone initiated, unless the government of a state of consequence conceives of the idea and concludes that the balance of interests of various states does not rule out the acceptance of neutralization.

There are three counterconsiderations which justify a less pessimistic conclusion about the utility of neutralization. First, though the difficulties of control and enforcement appear to be great regarding a particular area, they may not be insurmountable if the interests of the main parties to the agreement are sufficiently congruent. Second, to be useful as an instrument for regulating interstate violence, a neutralization agreement need not work perfectly or permanently. Even if a particular scheme has little prospect of working for more than ten or fifteen, or even five, years, it may still be very much worthwhile in terms of averting or moderating dangerous instability for a time. Moreover, whereas the failure of neutralization to prevent direct and large-scale military aggression is clear-cut and decisive—in the sense that

15

neutralization either works or does not—failure or success in stopping less direct forms of coercion, or irregular warfare, is a question of more or less. There can be degrees of success. Even if subversive activities from across the boundary are not stopped altogether, or at all times, a great deal may be gained in raising the threshold to such violations and keeping them within limits.

Third, whatever the difficulties of negotiating or enforcing neutralization, if they are surmounted and neutralization achieves at least a partial or temporary success, this outcome, and the labors producing it, must be compared with the consequences of alternative courses of action or of inaction. Is it better to abandon any attempt at controlling international violence and coercion? Is it better to leave indirect aggression a free rein rather than curb it, even if only partly or with uncertain prospects of success, by means of neutralization? Is it better for great powers to intervene on opposite sides and raise the specter of major war? Is it better to rely on the United Nations, which is so often paralyzed by dissension? In many situations, it seems, the prospects of neutralization may be poor, but they may be less poor than the likely alternatives.

Nor are alternative methods for regulating interstate violence without disadvantages. If neutralization fails to work in a particular instance, these other methods might likewise have failed, or they might have failed where neutralization is successful. After all, the balance of power has frequently not been capable of preventing weak states from being militarily attacked or from suffering intervention or other forms of outside coercion in its internal affairs. When a threat of counterintervention fails to deter intervention, the resultant risk is precisely a

16

reason for considering a more effective and less risky and costly method of control. Membership in an alliance or sphere of influence may conflict with a weak nation's desire for noninvolvement in the tensions and antagonisms existing between groups of aligned states. A protecting power may curtail the independence of its client. Reliance on protection from the United Nations or regional organizations may provide only a doubtful basis for security.

Despite the difficulties inherent in negotiating and enforcing neutralization and despite the disadvantages which it may confer on the parties to a neutralization treaty, neutralization looks as though it may be a serviceable instrument for controlling international violence and coercion, and hence for supporting international order, in the contemporary world. There should be no illusion that it might find worldwide application and thus become a global problem-solver. But here and there the conditions for its adoption and working may well emerge, if they have not already done so.

Specifically, neutralization may remove international violence and coercion from an area rife with instabilities and potential strife. It may moderate international coercion even if it cannot prevent or stop it altogether. And, by offering contending powers a compromise, especially a face-saving compromise, it may help to terminate international violence and coercion already in progress. It is, therefore, worth studying both from an analytical point of view and from the standpoint of concern with some of the substantive problems of the contemporary world.

CHAPTER II

THE HISTORICAL EXPERIENCE
WITH NEUTRALIZATION

The Neutralization of States

THE MAIN purpose of the neutralization of states today is to preserve peace by means of special agreements regarding states that are subjects of international controversy. The neutralization of states is concerned with actual or potential sources of conflict; it seeks to ensure by means of formal commitments that the neutralized states will cease to be sources of conflict.

The neutralization of states is only one of a number of applications of the concept of neutrality, and for the sake of clarity it should be distinguished from other uses of this concept. A *unilateral declaration of neutrality* on the part of a state by means of a constitutional or legislative act, often referred to as *self-neutralization,* does not constitute a status of permanent neutrality in international law unless it is accompanied by some form of international agreement or recognition. *Neutralism* and *nonalignment* represent less formal types of self-neutralization, expressed as statements of policy rather than as constitutional or legislative acts. There are also various forms of *demilitarization* and *international administration* of states and parts of states, territories, and waterways. These arrangements are sometimes referred to as neutralization, and they present problems concerning the definition and maintenance of international guarantees analogous to those that arise for neutralized states. These two forms of international guarantee differ, however, in that demilitarized states, "atom-free" zones, and parts of states, territories, and waterways placed under one form or another of international guarantee do not share the problems of political neutrality facing sovereign states that are neutralized. *Neutrality,* finally, is a policy of abstaining from participation in war between other states. Such a policy involves no international guarantees, and, unlike self-neutralization and neutralism, it normally refers to specific wars and is not set forth as a general principle applicable over a long period of time. The rights and responsibilities of neutral states, defined by the Hague Convention of 1907 and other documents, pertain in time of war also to states that are permanently neutralized.

The primary concern of this book is the international status of permanent, or perpetual, neutrality. Permanent neutrality is a status conferred by agreement with other states. It is normally formalized by a treaty under the terms of which the independence and territory of a neutralized state are permanently guaranteed by one or more other states, in return for an undertaking on the part of the neutralized state to abstain from participation in wars, or in alliances or other commitments that might lead to war. Permanent neutrality may also be achieved, however, by means other than a formal treaty of guarantee. The term "neutralization" is employed in this connection to include the creation of a status of permanent neutrality by a variety of forms of international recognition.

Since our purpose is to examine the historical experience of the neutralization of states in light of its relevance to contemporary problems, a distinction should be made between the principal examples of permanent neutrality and the exceptional and analogous cases that do not appear to have wide applicability.

The principal examples of permanent neutrality are Switzerland, Belgium, Luxembourg, Austria, and Laos. In considering these cases, one is immediately struck by their diversity. The neutralization of Switzerland in 1815 represented an international recognition and guarantee of what had in effect been a self-neutralized state in the seventeenth and eighteenth centuries. Belgium and Luxembourg conformed more closely to the classic concept of neutralization, although the latter was demilitarized under circumstances that left some doubt about the responsibilities of the guarantors. Austria is from a formal standpoint a self-neutralized state, but its neutralization was in fact the consequence of a bilateral agreement with the USSR, and it is implemented by an unprecedented form of international recognition. Laos, finally, is the only example of a state neutralized under terms set forth at considerable length in a document negotiated by the guarantor states, but the document is in the form of a declaration rather than a treaty designed for ratification.

Although none of these cases represents a model that could readily be applied to a contemporary problem, the experience with important aspects of neutralization that each provides nevertheless will have a bearing on new situations in which neutralization may prove to be applicable.[1]

[1] There is no recent monograph that does full justice to this subject. Among the available studies, see especially Cyrus French Wicker, *Neutralization* (London 1911); Karl Strupp, *Neutralisation, Befriedung, Entmilitarisierung* (Stuttgart 1933); Bernard Bacot, *Des neutralités durables: Origine, domaine et efficacité* (Paris 1945); and B. M. Klimenko, *Demilitarizatsiia i neitralizatsiia v mezhdunarodnom prave* (Moscow 1963).

SWITZERLAND

The tradition of neutrality has deep roots in the history of individual cantons and of the Swiss confederation itself. The term "neutrality" was first employed in an official document in 1536, but the origins of the official policy are usually traced to a declaration of the Federal Diet in 1674 to the effect that Switzerland intended to adopt "a neutral position" in the war between France and the Netherlands. This declaration was the product of a period in which Swiss statesmen, through the perpetual peace (1516–1798) with France and similar arrangements with other countries, sought to protect their country from entanglement in the recurring wars that were characteristic of the European balance of power system. The involvement of Switzerland in the European wars of 1798–1815 brought an end to this traditional form of self-neutralization and set the stage for the adoption of an international convention.

The contemporary Swiss status of permanent neutrality dates from the Act of Paris of November 20, 1815, in which Austria, France, Great Britain, Prussia, and Russia declared "their formal and authentic acknowledgment of the perpetual neutrality of Switzerland; and they guarantee to that country the integrity and inviolability of its territory. . . ." What is significant about this declaration is that it represented an "acknowledgment," or recognition, of the traditional Swiss policy of neutrality as it had been established between 1674 and 1798. Switzerland was not being required by the guaranteeing states to surrender certain aspects of its sovereignty as the price of independence or in the interest of the international balance of power. Rather, a preexisting Swiss policy of neutrality was being reestablished as a

21

permanent feature of the European system of states. To this extent the Swiss case is unique in the annals of the neutralization of states. In other respects, however, the Swiss experience during the revolutions of 1830 and 1847–1850 and the wars of 1859, 1870–1871, 1914–1918, and 1939–1945 resulted in some well-established principles and practices that have a general applicability.[2]

In the light of the Swiss experience it is instructive to examine the official interpretation of neutrality adopted by the Political Department of the Swiss government on November 26, 1954.[3] This document starts out by noting the essential difference between customary and permanent neutrality. The former involves only non-participation in a war between other states, whereas the latter requires a commitment to neutrality in time of peace as well as in time of war. Permanent neutrality may be declared unilaterally or guaranteed; the 1954 statement regards the Swiss case as a combination of both features, that is, as a case of unilaterally declared permanent neutrality subsequently guaranteed by the five great powers in 1815. The Swiss interpretation then goes on to expound the three principal obligations of a permanently neutral state in time of peace: to abstain from starting a war, to defend its neutrality, and to avoid

[2] Edgar Bonjour, *Swiss Neutrality: Its History and Meaning* (London 1946), and his more detailed *Geschichte der schweizerischen Neutralität: Drei Jahrhunderte eidgenössischer Aussenpolitik* (Basel 1946); Paul Guggenheim, *Traité de Droit International Public* (2 vols.; Geneva 1953–1954), II, 547–561; Jacques M. Vergotti, *La neutralité de la Suisse* (Lausanne 1954); Samuel Gonard, "Les décisions stratégiques du général," *Général Guisan, 1874–1960*, ed. André Guex (Lausanne 1960), 35–45; and Jon Kimche, *Spying for Peace: General Guisan and Swiss Neutrality* (3rd edn.; London 1962).

[3] "Conception officielle suisse de la neutralité," *Schweizerisches Jahrbuch für Internationales Recht*, XIV (1957), 195–199.

policies and actions that might on some future occasion involve it in hostilities.

From a political standpoint, a permanently neutral state must not adhere to any treaty, including defensive alliances, treaties of guarantee, and collective security arrangements. It must also, of course, not enter into military agreements with other states. This limitation on ties with other states is restricted to political commitments, however, and does not extend to treaties concluded for humanitarian or other nonpolitical purposes. In particular, the obligations of permanent neutrality do not entail moral neutrality. Nor do they apply to individuals or call for any limitations on the freedom of the press.

The Swiss interpretation devotes particular attention to the third set of obligations, which it characterizes as "secondary obligations." Participation of a permanently neutral state in international conferences and organizations depends on whether their purpose is predominantly political or predominantly economic, cultural, or technical. Participation in a conference or organization with universal membership is particularly questionable, in the Swiss view, because such membership would include representatives of rival political groupings which might be parties to possible conflicts. At the same time, a permanently neutral state has the right to offer its good offices or mediation even during hostilities, without having to fear that this act might be regarded as unfriendly by any of the belligerents.

From an economic standpoint, a permanently neutral state must not enter into a customs or economic unions which might in any way jeopardize its independence of political action. Should it do so, the neutral state might become dependent on its economic partner to the extent that even a treaty provision for automatic withdrawal in time of war would not protect it from political involvement.

The official Swiss interpretation of 1954 concludes by pointing out that, as limitations on the sovereignty of a permanently neutral state, the obligations of neutrality should be narrowly interpreted. When Switzerland undertakes policies that go beyond those called for by customary or permanent neutrality, they should be regarded not as the fulfillment of obligations but as measures designed to strengthen the confidence of belligerents in the institution of neutrality.

This official interpretation has been summarized in some detail because it reflects the experience of the country with the longest record of neutrality. This is not to say, however, that this interpretation is an accepted part of international practice or that all Swiss political leaders would adhere to it. Indeed, as noted below, the question of Switzerland's relationship to international organizations is a matter of particular debate among the Swiss themselves.

BELGIUM AND LUXEMBOURG

The neutralization of Belgium and Luxembourg was guaranteed by the same states that served as guarantors of Swiss neutrality, but in these cases neutralization was undertaken under different circumstances and ran a different course. The peoples of Belgium and Luxembourg were incorporated into the Netherlands in 1815 as a means of erecting a barrier against a possible resurgence of French aggression. They were restless under Dutch rule, however, and revolted in 1830. The great powers now faced the problem of preserving the effectiveness of the barrier while granting the independence of the rebellious minorities, and it was under these circumstances that they adopted the procedure of neutralization by international guarantee.

A treaty guaranteeing the perpetual neutrality of Belgium was drafted by a conference of the five powers in 1831. Owing to the intransigence of the Dutch, however, final arrangements for Belgian independence and neutralization were not concluded until 1839. Thereafter Belgium continued to play a critical role in the relations of France, Prussia, and Great Britain. In 1866 Napoleon III entered into negotiations with Bismarck with a view to the French annexation of Belgium in compensation for the unification of Germany. These inconclusive negotiations were made public by Bismarck three years later, and in August 1870 Great Britain concluded separate treaties with France and Prussia providing that, in the event that either state violated Belgian neutrality, Britain would assist the other in defending it. After the German Schlieffen Plan became known in 1904, Belgium undertook negotiations with Great Britain and France in preparation for the defense of its neutrality in the event of a German attack. When the German invasion finally occurred in 1914, France and Great Britain came to Belgium's defense.

Belgium had always tended to regard neutralization as an unjustified limitation on its sovereignty imposed as a condition of its independence; the First World War gave it an opportunity to free itself from this restraint. Under Article 31 of the Treaty of Versailles Germany agreed to the abrogation of the treaty of 1839, and the neutralization of Belgium was terminated.[4]

[4] Alexander Fuehr, *The Neutrality of Belgium* (New York 1915); Karl Strupp, *Die Neutralisation und die Neutralität Belgiens* (Gotha 1917); André Roussel Le Roy, *L'Abrogation de la neutralité de la*

The Grand Duchy of Luxembourg, a small country with a population of 285,000 in 1900, gained its independence in more gradual stages than Belgium. Its neutralization was guaranteed in 1867, at a time when the European states were adjusting themselves to the Prussian victory over Austria. The treaty neutralizing Luxembourg differed from the Belgian treaty of 1839 in three respects. First, there was from the start a difference of opinion among the guarantor states in regard to their obligations. The British government regarded the guarantee as collective only, maintaining that the guarantor states were not individually responsible for the defense of Luxembourg's neutrality. The other four guarantor states did not accept this view, but the conflict of opinion was never resolved. Second, Luxembourg, unlike Belgium, was demilitarized as well as neutralized. Third, the Grand Duchy retained special ties with the Netherlands. King William III of the Netherlands continued as Grand Duke of Luxembourg until 1890, when he died without leaving a male heir. He was succeeded as Grand Duke by the Duke of Nassau-Weilburg, who established a separate line of succession.

The German occupation of Luxembourg during the First World War, in contrast to that of Belgium, was concerned primarily with the transit by rail of troops and supplies, and it did not involve significant interference in the affairs of the civilian government. Indeed, the government of the Grand Duchy did not consider that its neutralization had been violated and did not sever relations with Germany. As a nonbelligerent, Luxembourg was not invited to the peace conference, nor did it

---

Belgique, ses causes et ses effets (Paris 1923); and William E. Lingelbach, "Belgian Neutrality: Its Origin and Interpretation," *American Historical Review*, XXXIX (October 1933), 48–72.

sign the Treaty of Versailles, which provided in Article 40 for German recognition of the abrogation of the treaty of 1867. The Grand Duchy did not recognize the abrogation of the treaty; indeed, it considered its neutralization to be in force until the Second World War. Upon succumbing to a second German invasion, however, the government of the Grand Duchy went into exile in Great Britain and in May 1940 formally abandoned its policy of neutrality. In 1948 the constitution of the Grand Duchy was amended for the purpose of deleting the references to perpetual neutrality which it had incorporated since its adoption in 1868.[5]

AUSTRIA

The case of Austria is in important respects unique, and it illustrates the variety of forms that neutralization can take. The idea of a status of permanent neutrality for Austria arose from the efforts of France, Great Britain, the United States, and the Soviet Union to find a basis for agreement on the conclusion of a State Treaty that would end the four-power occupation of Austria undertaken in 1945 and give that country independent statehood. Postwar Soviet policy had maintained that the four-power occupation of Austria should continue until a peace treaty was signed with Germany, but in 1954 the Soviet government raised the possibility of a neutralized Austria as a basis for giving the country its independence without upsetting the existing balance of power in Central Europe. The other three occupying states did not favor a formal neutralization under the guarantee of the powers on the model of Belgium and Luxembourg, so the following spring the USSR and

[5] Marcel Junod, *Die Neutralität des Grossherzogtums Luxemburg von 1867 bis 1948* (Luxembourg 1951).

27

Austria undertook to negotiate the issue on a bilateral basis.

The outcome of these negotiations was the Moscow Memorandum of April 15, 1955. Under the terms of this formal agreement, Austria accepted the obligation to practice permanent neutrality of the type maintained by Switzerland, to obtain from the Austrian parliament a commitment to permanent neutrality, to take appropriate measures to obtain international recognition of this neutral status, and to request and accept a guarantee by the four powers of the inviolability and integrity of the territory of the Austrian state. The Soviet Union, for its part, agreed to recognize the declaration of neutrality and to participate in a four-power guarantee of Austrian territory.

Having obtained Austria's acceptance of these conditions, the USSR agreed to the conclusion of the Austrian State Treaty, and it was signed on May 15, 1955. On October 26 of the same year the Austrian parliament enacted a Constitutional Federal Statute in which "Austria, of its own free will, declares herewith its permanent neutrality . . . [and] will never in the future accede to any military alliances nor permit the establishment of military bases of foreign states on its territory." Austrian neutrality was subsequently recognized by the four great powers and by the other states with which it maintains diplomatic relations.[6]

[6] Josef L. Kunz, "Austria's Permanent Neutrality," *American Journal of International Law*, L (1956), 418–425; V. N. Beletskii, *Sovetskii soiuz i Avstriia* (Moscow 1962); Gerald Stourzh, "Zur Entstehungsgeschichte des Staatsvertrages und der Neutralität Österreichs 1945–1955," *Österreichische Zeitschrift für Aussenpolitik*, V (1965), 301–336; William B. Bader, *Austria Between East and West, 1945–1955* (Stanford 1966), 184–209; and Alfred Verdross, *Die immerwährende Neutralität der Republik Österreich* (2nd edn.; Vienna 1966).

There are a number of ambiguities in the Austrian pattern of neutralization that give it an unprecedented character, for Austria was in effect self-neutralized as a result of an international commitment. Austria assumed the obligations of permanent neutrality "of its own free will," in the sense that it took this step after the signature of the State Treaty and without a treaty of guarantee. Austria was free, however, only to choose between continued occupation and permanent neutrality; it did not have the option of an independent foreign policy without obligations. The international commitment was made to only one state, the Soviet Union, but this was a formal and public commitment understood by the other three occupying states to form an essential condition of the peace settlement. Moreover, the Constitutional Federal Statute of Austria was formally recognized by all four signatories of the State Treaty and by many other states as well. This unprecedented form of international recognition was not, however, accompanied by a four-power guarantee of Austrian territory.

Austria seeks to pursue a policy based on the Swiss model, and as an example of permanent neutrality it occupies a position comparable to that of the other four states discussed here. The manner in which Austria achieved this status illustrates the variety of paths that can lead to permanent neutrality. It is not a path, however, that other states are likely to follow.

LAOS

The treaties providing for the neutralization of Switzerland, Belgium, and Luxembourg were guaranteed by the same five powers, inspired by a common political culture. The four occupying powers involved in the Austrian case, despite significant differences in policy, were in agreement that Austria should continue as a non-aligned state after independence. Laos, on the other hand, was guaranteed by a group of states in fundamental disagreement with each other over basic principles and policies. The guarantor states were all more or less involved in the internal affairs of Laos, and neutralization was proposed as a compromise solution to a complex international dispute.

The Declaration on the Neutrality of Laos was signed on July 23, 1962, by Burma, Cambodia, Canada, the People's Republic of China, the Democratic Republic of Vietnam, France, India, Poland, the Republic of Vietnam, Thailand, the Union of Soviet Socialist Republics, the United Kingdom, and the United States. The Declaration set forth the obligations of the Royal Government of Laos in detail much greater than in any preceding treaty of neutralization. It also assigned to the three-member Commission for Supervision and Control of Laos, established under the Geneva Agreement of 1954, the task of enforcing the neutralization of Laos. This Commission reports to the Co-Chairmen of the International Conference for the Settlement of the Laotian Question, 1961–1962, and their successors in the offices of the British Secretary of State for Foreign Affairs and the Soviet Minister of Foreign Affairs. France and the United States argued at the conference for a Commission with more effective powers, but their view was not accepted by the majority. The Commission is an instrument of the guarantor states; it serves as an extension of their collective authority within the territory of the neutralized state. Although the Commission has not been effective in controlling repeated interventions by several of the guarantor states, it does represent an important precedent in establishing the principle that guarantor states may set up a sizable and durable instrument to ensure the maintenance of a treaty of neutralization.[7]

Exceptional and Analogous Cases of Neutralization

There are several other cases of the neutralization of states, but these are of such a special or limited character that they do not constitute substantial precedents in the historical record. They nevertheless deserve brief mention:

Cracow, a city state, was neutralized by the treaty of September 6, 1815, signed by Austria, Prussia, and Russia. Its neutralized status lasted until 1846, when it was abrogated by agreement among the guarantor states and Cracow was annexed by Austria.

The Independent State of Congo was neutralized by the General Act of the Congress of Berlin, February 28, 1885. This neutralization was not guaranteed by the signatory states, however, and it was terminated with the annexation of Congo by Belgium in 1907.

Honduras was neutralized by the Central American Republics in a treaty signed on December 20, 1907. This treaty was abrogated in 1923.

Provision was made for the neutralization of Albania in a treaty of July 29, 1913, with Austria-Hungary, France, Germany, Great Britain, Italy, and Russia as the guarantor states. There was no further mention in the

[7] George Modelski, *International Conference on the Settlement of the Laotian Question, 1961–62* (Canberra 1962); John J. Czyzak and Carl F. Salans, "The International Conference on the Settlement of the Laotian Question and the Geneva Agreements of 1962," *American Journal of International Law,* LVII (April 1963), 300–317; O. N. Khlestov, "Zhenevskie soglasheniia po Laosu–vazhnyi shag v formirovanii sovremennogo poniatie neitraliteta," *Sovetskoe gosudarstvo i pravo* (1963), no. 5, 91–100; and Arthur J. Dommen, *Conflict in Laos: The Politics of Neutralization* (New York 1964).

public record of the neutralization of Albania, and it was allowed to lapse as a result of the war.

The Vatican City State, finally, was neutralized under the terms of a treaty concluded with Italy, the guarantor state, on February 11, 1929. This treaty is still in force.

There are a few cases of formal self-neutralization of states. Thus, Iceland, when it gained its independence from Denmark in 1918, declared itself to be "permanently neutral." Similarly, Cambodia, in 1957, adopted a Neutrality Law under which the government bound itself to abstain from all military or ideological alliances with other countries. Such unilateral assertions of neutralization embodied in domestic statutes are not binding in international law, and their political consequences vary with the circumstances.

It has also been common in recent years for states to make less formal declarations of "neutralism," "positive neutrality," and "nonalignment," normally in the form of a statement of intent not to enter into military or political alliances with other states. Such declarations have been made, for example, by Burma, India, Iraq, Sudan, the United Arab Republic, and Yugoslavia. Such declarations are not binding in international law and are regarded simply as statements of national policy.

There are a number of instances in which the neutralization, demilitarization, or international administration of parts of states—as well as of waterways and strategic areas, including outer space, that are not parts of states—overlap with the neutralization of states in matters of terminology and form that are frequently confusing. Strictly speaking, neutralization is concerned with the political aspects of foreign policy in general, whereas demilitarization is concerned with only those aspects of political power that involve the use of military weapons or forces.

The confusion arises from the fact that the various forms of demilitarization and international control of parts of states are often referred to as "neutralization," even though such territories do not have independent policies and demilitarization is in fact the most significant concern of the signatory states. When the term "neutralization" is employed in regard to states, it means that these states are obligated not to enter into political or military alliances with other states; when it is employed in regard to parts of states and other territories (the Antarctic, the moon, etc.), it means that the sovereignty of no one state will be permitted to prevail and that political matters are under the joint jurisdiction of the signatories. Territories that are internationally administered are normally demilitarized and "neutralized" in this limited sense.

In the cases of the neutralization of Malta (1802), Chablais and Faucigny (1815–1919), Moresnet (1816–1914), the Aaland Islands (since 1856), the Ionian Islands (1863–1891), the Samoan Islands (1886–1899), the Rhineland (1919–1935), the Saar territory (1919–1935), the Free City of Danzig (1919–1939), the International Zone of Tangier (1923–1940, 1945–1956), and the Free Territory of Trieste (1945–1954), general political as well as military considerations were involved. Similarly, in the rather special case of the neutralization of the Antarctic in 1959 under the guarantee of twelve states with interests in that region, concern regarding the use of the Antarctic for military purposes was combined with considerations of political jurisdiction and of economic and scientific interests. The various proposals and agreements regarding the use of international waterways, such as the Black Sea, the Rhine and Danube rivers, the Straits of Magellan, the Danish and Turkish straits, and the Suez and Panama canals, have generally involved elements of neutralization and demilitarization among other considerations. The study of such cases is relevant to the neutralization of states insofar as they illustrate the constituent factors in the viability and effectiveness of regimes of neutralization.

Demilitarization in a narrower sense has been discussed on a number of occasions as a means of limiting the use of nuclear weapons. A widely discussed proposal of this type was the Rapacki Plan. In October 1957 the Polish foreign minister urged that Poland, Czechoslovakia, the German Democratic Republic, and the German Federal Republic impose a ban on the production and stockpiling of nuclear weapons in their territories and that France, Great Britain, the USSR, and the United States assume the obligation not to introduce nuclear weapons into this "atom-free" zone. The Rapacki Plan was revised in November 1958 to include a withdrawal of foreign troops from the territory of the countries of this zone. These proposals were rejected by the Western governments on the grounds that the size of the Soviet conventional forces available for deployment in Central Europe would give the USSR a decisive preponderance in conventional military power in the absence of nuclear weapons and that the plan would result in a decisive increase in Soviet influence in this region as compared with the existing situation. In neither version of this plan was neutralization proposed in the sense of restricting the right of Czechoslovakia, Poland, and the two Germanies to enter into alliances with other countries. It was assumed that the German Federal Republic would continue to be a member of NATO and the other three countries members of the Warsaw Pact.

A number of other proposals for the creation of "atom-free" zones in various parts of the world have been advanced as a means of limiting the proliferation of nuclear weapons. Such proposals have little direct bearing on the neutralization of states by international guarantee. Similarly, the Treaty Banning Nuclear Weapons Tests in the Atmosphere, in Outer Space, and Underwater (1963) and the Treaty on Principles Governing the Activities of States in the Exploration and Use of Outer Space, including the Moon and other Celestial Bodies (1966), are essentially concerned with demilitarization.

The Effectiveness of Neutralization

The guarantor states have normally played the principal role in the initiation, maintenance, and termination of treaties for the neutralization of states. Neutralization is a device to defuse situations involving international conflict. The initiative taken by guarantor states in drafting treaties of neutralization reflects their interest in removing a potential source of conflict by means of a compromise.

The guarantor states have normally been responsible for the maintenance of neutralization, as an obligation assumed by virtue of their guarantee. The form of the guarantee is usually joint-and-several; in other words, each guarantor is free to intervene independently to defend the neutralized state in the event that a joint policy cannot be agreed upon by the guarantors. There have been exceptions to this practice, however. With regard to the treaty of 1867 guaranteeing the neutrality of Luxembourg, the British government maintained that the guarantee was collective only, that individual guarantors were not obligated to act if unanimity could not be achieved. The other guarantors, however, did not accept the British interpretation. In the case of the Congo, the guarantee was individual rather than collective, and its primary purpose was to assure equal opportunities for commerce.

In practice it has been the balance of power among the major guarantors, rather than any formal machinery, that has ensured the success of neutralization. Thus, Germany and France respected Swiss and Belgian neutrality in the war of 1870–1871 because the costs in terms of the enmities that might have been aroused on the part of other states were regarded as greater than the advantages that might have been gained by violating their neutrality. In the First World War, again, although the German general staff entertained the possibility of attacking France through Switzerland, it estimated the cost to be greater than possible gains. Germany made a different calculation in regard to Belgium and Luxembourg in 1914, and the enmity aroused by its violation of the neutralization treaties was a significant factor in rallying the coalition of states that finally brought about Germany's defeat.

The neutralization of a state by international guarantee does not provide automatic assurance that the guarantee will be observed, but it does raise the cost of aggression to a higher degree than exists where there is no international guarantee. The nature of this cost will certainly fluctuate as the relations of the guarantors and their real power evolve over the years. Yet the very fact that a treaty of neutralization has been agreed upon reflects a commitment, based on the national interests of the guarantor states, which normally offers promise of considerable stability.

The guarantor states have also normally taken the initiative in terminating neutralization treaties when in their opinion conditions have changed sufficiently to warrant such an action. The defeat of Germany in 1918, for instance, was considered by the victorious states to make the neutralization of Belgium and Luxembourg no longer necessary, and clauses were included in the Treaty of Versailles abrogating these two treaties. Similarly, the neutralization of the Republic of Cracow was terminated in 1846 by the decision of the guarantor states. In the analogous cases of neutralization of parts of states, territories, and waterways, the initiative is always taken by one or more of the guarantor states since the objects of neutralization have no sovereignty.

Only exceptionally have all the guarantor states had an equal interest in the maintenance of the neutralization of a state, and it has generally been assumed that a few main guarantors with effective power accessible to the guaranteed state will have the principal interest in, and bear the main burden of, maintaining neutralization. Thus, although Russia had played a major military role in Western Europe during the Napoleonic Wars and was a guarantor of the neutralization of Switzerland, Belgium, and Luxembourg, it did not actually have any direct interest in these states as France, Germany, and Great Britain did, and its role in maintaining their neutralization was accordingly minor. So, too, of the thirteen states that guaranteed the neutralization of Laos, only three or four had the practical means of defending (or threatening) it. At the other extreme, the Vatican City State forms an enclave within the territory of the single guarantor of its neutralization.

The sovereignty of all states is affected when they sign a treaty, insofar as they surrender their freedom of action for the purposes and duration of the treaty. A neutralized state surrenders more freedom of action than is called for by most treaties in that it gives up as a minimum the right to enter into alliances with other states and, hence, to safeguard its international existence by its own action. The example of Luxembourg notwithstanding, neutralized states do, of course, normally retain the right to maintain armies. Yet they cannot serve as guarantors of other neutralized states. Thus, although Belgium was a signatory to the treaty neutralizing Luxembourg, it could not serve as a guarantor. It is, further, a matter of dispute whether, and to what extent, neutralized states may participate in global and regional international organizations. Apart from these limitations on their sovereignty, however, neutralized states have all the rights and responsibilities of other states. At the same time, because of the nature of their status, neutralized states have not normally played an independent role in the initiation, maintenance, and termination of neutralization.

A notable exception to this rule is Switzerland. The formal initiative in establishing the principle of neutralization for Switzerland in 1815 was taken by the five guarantor states, with particular attention to the balance of power between France and Austria. Yet the principle of neutrality, as distinct from the particular form of neutralization adopted in 1815, was one that already had firm roots in Swiss policy. To this extent the neutralization was more a formalization of existing Swiss policy than the creation of a new policy by the guarantor states.

The evolution of the policies associated with Swiss

neutralization after 1815 reveal the relative importance of the guaranteed state in comparison with other cases of the neutralization of states. In the negotiations regarding Neuchatel, which lasted from 1848 to 1857, it was essentially the determination of the Swiss government—strongly supported by France, to be sure—that finally led to the renunciation by Prussia of its traditional sovereignty over the Swiss canton. At the start of the wars of 1859, 1870–1871, 1914–1918, and 1939–1945, Switzerland supplemented the treaty guarantees by separate declarations of neutrality that gave notice of its determination to remain aloof from the wars that engulfed its neighbors. A significant factor in the success of Switzerland in defending its status of permanent neutrality, particularly during the two World Wars, was its own military readiness. Although the Swiss military establishment was relatively small, it was sufficiently well organized so that none of the belligerents could hope to invade Switzerland without withdrawing sizable forces from other sectors of the front. As time passed, the role of Switzerland as a center of international finance and commerce and as headquarters for a wide variety of international organizations served to reinforce its neutralization. A potential aggressor had to consider not only the significant military costs of violating Swiss neutrality but also the loss of Swiss financial and commercial services and the enmity of many other countries that depended on Switzerland for these services.

In contrast to this active role of Switzerland in the maintenance of its permanent neutrality, the guarantor states did not maintain the interest that had stimulated their original support of neutralization in 1815. Russia never had a major interest in Switzerland, and after the revolution in 1917 it was not until 1946 that it even reestablished diplomatic relations. The role of Austria declined rapidly after its defeat in 1859, and, indeed, it declared its own neutralization in 1955. France, Germany, and Great Britain retained their active interest in the neutralization of Switzerland, but Germany was at war with France in 1870–1871 and with both of its coguarantors in 1914–1918 and 1939–1945. It cannot therefore be maintained that the success of Swiss neutralization has been due to the initiative of the guarantor states; it would be more correct to say that it has been successful in spite of them. Indeed, although from a strictly legal point of view the neutral status of Switzerland is based on the treaty of 1815, from a practical standpoint it is an example of self-neutralization rather than of neutralization by international guarantee. In any event, the example of Switzerland is unique in the history of the neutralization of states and must be regarded less as a model for the future than as an exceptional case that is not likely to be duplicated.

In evaluating the evidence provided by historical precedents in regard to the effectiveness of permanent neutrality, the essential consideration is the extent to which neutralization has provided a framework for a compromise settlement of controversial issues.

Neutralization is relevant in those circumstances where a conflict of interests exists. Given such a conflict of interests, the effect of a treaty of neutralization by international guarantee is to establish in legally binding terms the fact that the guarantor states would rather sacrifice the option of intervening in the affairs of the guaranteed state than permit an unstable situation to continue in which one or more of the interested states may threaten the peace by undertaking unilateral or competitive intervention. The effectiveness of neutralization should therefore be judged by the extent to which treaties of neutralization have served to provide solutions to controversial situations.

It is pertinent to note in this connection that, of the states neutralized in the last century, Switzerland has retained this status for 153 years (1815–1968), while Belgium remained neutral for 80 years (1839–1919) and Luxembourg for 52 years (1867–1919). Of the neutralization treaties concluded in the twentieth century, that of the Vatican City State has lasted 39 years (1929–1968) and that of Laos 6 years (1962–1968). One should also bear in mind that the neutralizations of Cracow, Congo, and Honduras remained in force for 31, 23, and 16 years, respectively, and were terminated by agreement among the guarantors. Moreover, the analogous forms of the neutralization of parts of states, territories, and waterways have endured for substantial periods despite the presence of international rivalries.

Even after removing the Swiss case from consideration, because of its exceptional character, the remaining cases of the neutralization of states give evidence of a significant viability. The neutralizations of Belgium and Luxembourg survived not only a major war between France and Germany, in 1870–1871, but half a century of intense national rivalry on the part of the principal guarantors. They succumbed only in the course of a major world war that marked a complete reorientation of relations among European states.

It would be extravagant to expect that treaties neutralizing states by international guarantee would survive a period in which the guarantor states were prepared to seek fulfillment of their national interests by means of total war. The function of such treaties is rather to mitigate the divisive effects of controversial situations, to reduce the incidence of local wars, and to provide compromise solutions of conflicts that might generate major wars. To achieve this purpose in a rapidly changing world a treaty of neutralization need not be "permanent" in order to be effective. A neutralization that resolves a difficult problem for a period of twenty to fifty years may well constitute a vital contribution to the maintenance of peace.

CHAPTER III

NEUTRALIZED STATES AND INTERNATIONAL RELATIONS

IN CONSIDERING the alternative roles that might be played by permanently neutral states in the international system, several matters deserve careful examination. The historical experience with permanent neutrality is limited, and, in effect, within the international system that has evolved since the Second World War the only examples are Switzerland, Austria, and Laos—the case of the Vatican City State being too far removed from the sphere of international relations to be relevant in this context.

The relationship of Switzerland and Austria to the international system has been a matter of active debate in recent years, and their experience is significant as representing a pragmatic point of departure for an examination of this subject. These specific cases raise questions of principle and policy that have a long history in the deliberations of political leaders and specialists in international law and relations. It is therefore important to review the principal conceptions of neutralization and permanent neutrality that inform the discussion of this subject today.

Prevailing Attitudes Toward Neutralization

Attitudes of political leaders in major states toward the proper role in contemporary international relations of the neutralization of states by international guarantee, and of related forms of neutralization, reflect three reasonably distinct approaches: that of the West European states, that of the Soviet Union, and that of the United States.

WESTERN EUROPE

The experience of the West European states with permanent neutrality dates from the beginning of the nineteenth century. For much of the period between the Napoleonic Wars and the First World War, France, Germany, and Great Britain relied on treaties of neutralization to protect their interests in the strategically pivotal regions of Switzerland, Belgium, and Luxembourg. These arrangements provided security in these critical areas during a period in which the entire European system of states was being reorganized, and the neutralization of Switzerland survived even the two world wars of the twentieth century in the course of which all other bulwarks of European security collapsed.

The West European states have in the light of this experience adopted a generally positive view of neutralization as a means of managing power with respect to countries and areas in dispute; in fact, they have been responsible for initiating most of the international agreements providing for neutralization in various forms of parts of states, waterways, and other strategic regions. The employment of neutralization by West European states has been for the purpose of maintaining the balance of power, primarily among themselves, and it has thus been regarded as a device for preserving the status quo. The conceptions of a concert of Europe and a balance of power have predominated in this attitude, and neutralization has been seen as a means of avoiding controversies that might upset such a balance. The West

44

European states view the permanent neutrality of Switzerland as a positive contribution to European security and that of Austria as a logical way of solving a critical problem. West European statesmen are also inclined to turn readily to neutralization as a solution to similar problems in other parts of the world.[1]

SOVIET UNION

The Soviet attitude toward neutralization differs from that of the West European states primarily in that it takes neutralization to be a means of changing the balance of power rather than of preserving it. International law is interpreted in the Soviet Union in terms of "the principle of peaceful coexistence." This principle embraces several concepts, of which the chief ones are the acceptance of the USSR by other leading states as an equal partner in the solution of international problems, the resolution of conflicts between the major states without resort to war, and the transformation of all societies from "feudalism" through "capitalism" to "socialism" and "communism," in the sense that these terms are used in Marxism–Leninism. Neutrality, neutralization, and neutralism relate to the principle of peaceful coexistence insofar as they serve to weaken the association of states under "capitalist" leadership and thereby create more favorable conditions for the transfer of societies to "socialist" influence.[2]

Soviet international law subscribes to a version of the

[1] The traditional West European view is summarized in Malbone W. Graham, Jr., "Neutralization as a Movement in International Law," *American Journal of International Law*, XXI (January 1927), 79–94; and in the literature on the permanent neutrality of Switzerland and Austria.

[2] F. I. Kozhevnikov, ed., *Mezhdunarodnoe pravo* (Moscow 1964), 81–93.

theory of just and unjust wars according to which wars waged against aggression and wars of national liberation are regarded as just. Since the semantics of this theory is that of Marxism–Leninism, "unjust" wars are those with which capitalist states are associated, and "just" wars are those initiated or supported by Soviet policy. In the framework of this Marxist–Leninist point of view, neutralization—along with neutrality and neutralism—is seen primarily as a method of drawing states away from, or preventing them from being drawn into, the orbit of "aggressive military blocs of imperialist states"—of which NATO is the leading example. A policy of nonparticipation in military blocs is regarded as a means of supporting peace and preventing war. Neutral states are not neutral so far as the issue of war and peace is concerned but struggle actively for peace by seeking to foil the plans of "imperialist aggressors." [3]

The USSR is not inclined to make sharp distinctions between the neutralization of states by international guarantee and other forms of neutralization, since all are directed toward the same goal. Traditionally neutral policies such as that of Sweden, proposals for demilitarization such as the Rapacki Plan, and other proposals for "atom-free" zones are treated as part of the same general category as the neutralization of states.

Soviet policy favors the example of Switzerland, which was cited explicitly as the model for Austrian neutrality in the Moscow Memorandum of 1955. It also regards the neutralization of Laos in 1962 as a model that other states should follow. The proposal of the Dutch Communist Party in 1962 that the Netherlands withdraw from NATO and proclaim its neutrality is also cited as correct com-

[3] Kozhevnikov, 604, 630–631.

munist tactics. Soviet authorities envisage a general policy of neutralization embracing the Balkan and Scandinavian states, Japan, the Philippines, and other states in East Asia, and the states of Latin America and Africa.[4]

At the same time, Soviet policy opposes the neutralization of any state associated with the USSR. Under the Rapacki Plan the demilitarization of Poland, Czechoslovakia, and the German Democratic Republic was accepted as the price for the demilitarization of the German Federal Republic, but it was not proposed that these states be neutralized in the sense of requiring them to withdraw from their commitments to the USSR and to the Warsaw Pact. The Marxist-Leninist attitude toward neutralization is thus one that sees it as one aspect of the transition from "capitalism" to "socialism." Neutralization removes or withholds states from the "capitalist" grouping and can to this extent reduce the resistance of their leaders to measures in the political, economic, and social spheres designed to promote "socialism" in their societies.

UNITED STATES

Although there is no formal statement of the United States covering the general subject of neutralization, the development of its policy in this regard may be deduced from a series of specific acts and statements. Before the Second World War the main concern of the United States for the principle of neutrality was with the development

---

[4] In addition to Klimenko, cited in Chap. II, note 1, see V. N. Durdenevskii, "Neitralitet v sisteme kollektivnoi bezopastnosti," *Sovetskoe Gosudarstvo i Pravo* (1957), no. 8, 81–91; A. Galina, "Problema neitraliteta v sovremennom mezhdunarodnom prave," *Sovetskoi Ezhegodnik Mezhdunarodnogo Prava, 1958* (Moscow 1959), 200–229; B. V. Ganiushkin, *Neitralitet i neprisoedinenie* (Moscow 1965); and H. Fiedler, *Der sowjetische Neutralitäts-begriff in Theorie und Praxis* (Köln 1959).

of its own policies as a neutral. It was, in fact, the principal exponent of the laws of neutrality before its entry into the First World War and from the passage of the Neutrality Act of 1935 until 1941. This attitude was based in part on a desire to avoid being drawn into the two world wars and in part on a traditional policy of shunning foreign entanglements that can be traced back to Washington's Farewell Address (1796).[5]

Since the Second World War the United States has relied for its security on the Charter of the United Nations and on collective defense arrangements under Article 51 of the Charter, among which are included some forty-two alliance treaties that form the NATO, CENTO, SEATO, and OAS groupings. It is the view of the United States that, since members of the United Nations are enjoined by the terms of the Charter from using force or threat of force against any state, neutrality in its various forms is in principle redundant. The United States has tended, moreover, to regard neutrality, neutralization, and neutralism as obstacles to its collective defense system.

Within this general framework of a policy hostile to neutralization, however, the United States has supported it in those cases where the interested states have reached a mature decision that it is the best means of dealing with a specific situation. Thus, the United States was a signatory of the agreements neutralizing the international zone of Tangier (1945–1956) and the Free Territory of Trieste (1945–1954), of the Antarctic Treaty (1959), and of the Declaration on the Neutrality of Laos (1962). In the course of the negotiations at Geneva concerning Laos,

---

[5] The most comprehensive statement of the traditional United States policy is in Philip C. Jessup *et al., Neutrality: Its History, Economics and Law* (4 vols.; New York 1935–1936).

Secretary of State Dean Rusk made a strong statement supporting the neutralization of Laos and stressing the need for "positive assurance of the integrity of elements of the national life" and "effective international machinery for maintaining and safeguarding that neutrality against threats to it from within as well as from without." [6]

The United States has usually favored a legalistic position in regard to international treaties of neutralization and has maintained that such treaties do not have consequences for nonsignatory states. The United States never recognized in a formal sense the neutralization of Switzerland, Belgium, and Luxembourg. After the entry of the United States into the First World War, however, it informed Switzerland that it would observe its neutrality as long as it was respected by the enemy.

In a similar spirit, the United States has not regarded domestic legislation proclaiming self-neutralization, such as that of Austria and Cambodia, as binding on other states. This position is defined in a memorandum on the "Nature of Austria's Neutrality and Legal Implication of United States Response to the Neutrality Declaration," dated November 16, 1955, by the Office of the Legal Adviser of the Department of State. This memorandum reviews the opinions of leading authorities and points out that a nonparticipating state may recognize a treaty of neutralization or a declaration of self-neutralization in the sense of declaring that as a matter of policy it will not violate the neutrality, but that it has no commitment to defend such neutralization unless it has explicitly agreed to guarantee it. Thus, when the United States

[6] "United States Outlines Program to Insure Genuine Neutrality for Laos. Statement by Secretary Rusk," *Department of State Bulletin,* XLIV (June 5, 1961), 846.

informed Austria in a note dated December 6, 1955, that it "recognizes the perpetual neutrality of Austria . . ." it was simply announcing its intention to refrain from taking actions that might violate Austria's neutrality.[7]

The support of the neutralization of Laos, the only case where the United States has served as a guarantor of a state neutralized by international guarantee, establishes a new precedent for United States policy. It remains to be seen whether this will remain a unique exception, attributable to unusual circumstances unlikely to be repeated, or whether it actually represents a change in policy due to a growing concern for the avoidance of conflicts on the borders of the American and Soviet collective defense systems. The American contribution to the neutralization of Laos, in collaboration with France, was the proposal that effective enforcement machinery be set forth in detail in the treaty. Although the Franco-American proposals were not adopted, the Laotian treaty shows the effects of this concern in that it is the first treaty of neutralization in which the obligations of both guaranteed and guarantor states are set forth in such detail.

Neutralized States and International Organizations

The limitation on permanently neutral states that they may conduct no military operations other than those concerned with the defense of their neutrality and may enter into no alliances with other states has raised the question of their relationship to global and regional international organizations that have a military or political character. This problem did not arise until the establishment of

---

[7] Marjorie M. Whiteman, ed., *Digest of International Law* (Washington, D.C. 1963–   ), I, 342–364.

the League of Nations, but the growing role of international organizations in recent years has given it increasing importance.

UNITED NATIONS

The essential elements of the problem emerged in 1920 when the question of Swiss membership in the League of Nations arose. The Covenant of the League, in Article 16, provided that, if a member state were to have recourse to war, the other members would be obligated to apply sanctions, including the severance of commercial and financial relations and the permission for passage through its territory of troops directed against the aggressor. Since this requirement is clearly incompatible with the obligations of a permanently neutral state, the League decided to make an exceptional arrangement for Switzerland in order that it might join the organization. The League decided in 1920 that Switzerland would be bound to participate in economic sanctions applied by the League but, as an exceptional case, would not be called upon to participate in military action or to permit the use of its territory for the transit of foreign troops or for the preparation of military operations authorized by the League. This compromise arrangement was referred to as "differential" or "qualified" neutrality. Switzerland joined the League under these exceptional conditions and participated in its affairs for over a decade, but it became uneasy when the system of collective security began to lose its effectiveness in the 1930s. A Swiss request to the League for release from the obligation to participate in economic sanctions was granted in 1938, and the "integral" or "unqualified" neutrality of Switzerland was restored for the remaining period of the League's activity.

Although the Charter of the United Nations is more flexible than the Covenant of the League of Nations in its demands on member states for sanctions against aggressors, there are nevertheless serious problems regarding the compatibility of membership in the United Nations with a status of permanent neutrality. The Charter provides in Article 43 that member states may be called upon by the Security Council to apply economic and diplomatic sanctions and also to take military measures against any state found guilty of a breach of the peace or of an act of aggression.

When the United Nations was established, the Swiss government studied the provisions of the Charter and concluded that the only type of membership compatible with its status of neutralization would be the same type of exceptional membership that the League granted it in 1938. The Swiss government decided, however, not to make such an application. This decision was presumably reached in the belief that the United Nations would not be inclined to admit Switzerland to a form of membership that would free it from the responsibilities assumed by the other member states.[8] At the end of the Second World War the principles of neutralization, neutrality, and neutralism were held in very low esteem by the states which had made such great sacrifices to win the war and which regarded the commitment to fight against dictatorship as a higher value than neutrality. Indeed, it was one of the conditions of admission to the San Francisco Conference in 1945, at which the Charter of the United Nations was adopted, that states demonstrate their desire for peace by declaring war on Germany and its allies.

[8] Reinhart Ehni, *Die Schweiz und die Vereinten Nationen von 1944–1947* (Tübingen 1967).

Even though Switzerland has not become a member of the United Nations, however, it has participated in many of its activities. Besides having a permanent Swiss observer stationed at the United Nations headquarters, Switzerland has contributed to the work of the UN in its role as a member of UNESCO, the Food and Agriculture Organization, the World Meteorological Organization, the International Atomic Energy Agency, and other bodies created by and affiliated with the United Nations. It has provided two chairmen of UNICEF, two UN High Commissioners for Refugees, and substantial funds and personnel for the United Nations Development Fund. In the realm of peacekeeping, Switzerland not only has served as a member of the UN Armistice Commission for Korea but in 1956 transported Italian UN contingents to Egypt on Swiss aircraft at its own expense and, at the time of the UN intervention in Congo, sent Swiss specialists to participate in a civilian capacity in the work to be done there. In addition, Switzerland made a loan to the United Nations when it suffered its financial crisis and also contributed to the financing of the UN peacekeeping forces in Cyprus. All of these activities have been regarded by the Swiss government as in no way incompatible with its policy of permanent neutrality.

An examination of the experience of the twenty years since the establishment of the United Nations has raised in Swiss governing circles the question whether regular membership in that organization as it has worked out in practice would in fact be incompatible with the Swiss tradition and policy of neutrality. The original negative decision in 1945 was reached on the basis of advice by experts who based their opinion on the wording of the Charter alone, since there was at the time no experience to guide them, but in the course of two decades the

United Nations has proved to be substantially different in practice from what it appeared to be in theory in 1945.[9]

The case can be made, for example, that in practice member states have not been required to take up arms against aggressors and that a substantial share of peace-keeping activity has been transferred from the Security Council to the General Assembly where no decisions are binding upon members. When the Security Council itself has taken the initiative, as in the case of Congo and Cyprus, the peacekeeping forces have been sent from contingents contributed voluntarily by member states. The financing of peacekeeping activities has also tended to become voluntary.

It remains the view of the Swiss government that a collective security system with mandatory participation in coercive measures of a military, political, economic, and financial character is not compatible with a policy of neutrality. At the same time, practice has shown that the United Nations is not as rigid in this respect as the League of Nations was. Military sanctions under Article 43 of the Charter depend on a consensus of the permanent members of the Security Council, and in over twenty years they have never been able to agree on such a measure. If they were to agree, the decision would not be binding on all members, and the Security Council would be free to decide which members it should invite to undertake a specific action. Within such a framework of obligations it would be possible for a member state to maintain a policy of neutrality. In the event that the General Assembly rather than the Security Council

[9] See especially the speech of the Swiss Federal Counsellor W. Spühler, "La Suisse et les Nations Unies" (mimeographed) of October 21, 1966.

were to undertake collective security action, its decisions would not be mandatory, and a neutral state would have the option to abstain from participation.

Apart from specific measures relating to collective security, however, a wide variety of political, economic, and social issues arise in the General Assembly, in regard to which the major groupings of states are inclined to take fixed and antagonistic positions. In some instances even a formal abstention could be interpreted as taking sides. The question would thus arise how far a neutral state would wish to go on the continuum extending from abstention from military coercive measures to abstention from expressing opinions about the many petty disputes of substance and procedure that mark the course of United Nations meetings.

It is relevant to note in this connection that Austria was accepted as a member of the United Nations after it had adopted a constitutional law asserting its perpetual neutrality. Similarly, the neutralization of Laos in 1962 has not been regarded as affecting its membership in the United Nations. It is at the same time significant that these decisions—acceptance as a member in the case of Austria and continuation of membership in the case of Laos—were taken without formal discussion of the compatibility between neutralization and membership. This is a question less of negligence on the part of the member states than of their conception of neutrality and neutralization. To the Swiss, neutrality is a national policy of avoiding all military and political commitments to foreign states. In the cases of Austria and Laos, by contrast, neutralization is a policy arising from the postwar balance of power between the two major collective defense systems. Apart from this predominant obligation to remain neutral in the rivalry between two coalitions,

Austria and Laos consider themselves free to participate in the normal business of the United Nations.

EUROPEAN ECONOMIC COMMUNITY

The relationship of neutralized states to the European Economic Community has been the second main problem facing them as members of the international system. The membership of Switzerland and Austria in the European Free Trade Association did not present a problem, because it involved only commercial relations. The EEC, on the other hand, not only has aspirations toward political integration but is also viewed by the USSR as a hostile coalition.

In 1961, at the time of the first British application, both Switzerland and Austria applied for associate membership in the EEC. With the rejection of the British application, however, the EEC postponed consideration of the question of the enlargement of the organization to include other major trading states. The admission of Greece, Turkey, and Nigeria to associate membership, it was felt, did not involve this larger question.

The Swiss interest in association with the EEC is motivated primarily by commercial considerations. It is the Swiss view that the main emphasis in EEC policy as it has developed since 1958 has been on economic rather than political integration and that it is in the interest of Switzerland to maintain the best possible bargaining position in commercial matters. Although participation in a politically integrated Europe might not be compatible with Swiss neutrality, this question would not be raised by associate membership in a Community in which the goal of political integration has receded into the distance. The Swiss government is therefore awaiting the further development of British efforts to join the EEC, as a necessary first step in the expansion of the Community.[10]

In contrast to the official Swiss attitude toward the EEC, there is a body of opinion in Switzerland that is hostile to the EEC in principle. This school of thought maintains that the EEC was established to meet the needs of the original six members and that it tends to foster domination by the central government over local authorities within each member state and domination of the smaller states by the larger within the organization. Swiss interests, in this view, do not require this type of protection. Swiss participation in the EEC could be purchased only at the high price of a subordination of its interests to those of the larger European states and of a threat to the traditional decentralized political and administrative structure of Switzerland. In any event, this question, unlike that of Swiss membership in the United Nations, is not one of reconciling Swiss neutrality with association with the EEC. Advocates of a Swiss relationship with the EEC are concerned simply with matters of trade and do not believe that significant political commitments would be involved.[11]

The question of the participation of Austria in the European Economic Community has been discussed along different lines, owing to the special character of Austria's permanent neutrality. The Austrian government maintains that it is free to join any international organization so long as it does not have a military character and that an association with the EEC is entirely compatible with

[10] Henri Stranner, *Neutralité suisse et solidarité européenne* (2nd edn.; Lausanne 1960); Henri Rieben, *La Suisse et le Marché Commun* (Lausanne 1960); and Wilhelm Röpke, Bernhard Wehrli, and Hans Haug, *Die Schweiz und die Integration des Westens* (Zurich 1965).

[11] Kurt Brotbeck, *Die schweizerische Neutralität als Beitrag zu einem freien Europa* (Bern 1963), 71–78.

its self-neutralization. In line with this interpretation, Austria revived its application in 1963, and the EEC agreed to undertake negotiations with a view to admitting it into some sort of association. It has been suggested that two conditions be accepted by Austria in the light of its neutralization: that it withdraw automatically from association with the EEC in the event of a war involving one of its members; and that it retain the freedom to dissociate itself from individual decisions of the EEC that it considers to be in violation of its neutrality.

The Soviet government has reacted strongly against this interpretation of Austrian neutrality, insisting that neutrality is indivisible. A neutralized state should refrain not only from entering into military alliances but also from all acts of a political, economic, or cultural nature that might favor one grouping of countries rather than another. Under this Soviet interpretation, there can be no question of a neutralized Austria associating itself with the European Economic Community. This argument is not without its weaknesses, however. Austria might negotiate a relationship with the EEC that was purely commercial, involving no greater commitments than membership in the EFTA. Alternatively, Switzerland might reach an agreement with the EEC, whereupon Austria could point to the Moscow Memorandum, which proposes Swiss neutrality as the model for Austria. Apparently to meet such objections, Soviet authorities have advanced the further argument that the Austrian State Treaty prohibits any form of economic union (*Anschluss*) between Austria and Germany. Since the German Federal Republic is a member of the EEC, this restriction on Austria is held to bar its entry into association with the whole Community.

The problem faced by Austria in regard to the EEC is thus both legal and political. The legal problem is to reconcile a possible relationship with the EEC to the constitutional law on neutrality. The political problem is Austria's concern that its relations with the USSR and Eastern Europe, including substantial trade, might be seriously affected if it overrode Soviet objections and concluded an agreement with the EEC.

Neutralization and the International System

NEUTRALIZATION AND WORLD POLITICS

In evaluating alternative policies of neutralization, it is important to distinguish between the technical aspects and the political consequences of neutralization. From a technical standpoint, a neutralized state is removed from international controversy by the obligation to abstain from military and political commitments to other states. The political significance of the neutralization of a state, on the other hand, is a separate question and depends on the political context in which neutralization takes place.

This proposition may be illustrated with reference to the historical examples of neutralization. The neutralization of Switzerland in 1815 and of Belgium in 1839 were, from a political standpoint, measures taken to safeguard against a renewal of the French territorial expansion that had taken place during the wars of 1793–1815. As late as 1859 France was regarded as the principal potential threat to Swiss neutrality. With the unification of the German-speaking peoples under Prussian leadership, however, the new Germany came to be looked upon as the power against which the restraints of neutralization were needed. Prussia threatened Swiss neutrality in

1847–1851, and the expansion of Germany became the principal reason for the neutralization of Luxembourg in 1867 and the reaffirmation of the neutralized status of Belgium in 1870. From the British standpoint, the neutralization of Belgium and, to a lesser extent, that of Luxembourg were related to the aim of protecting the security of Great Britain by ensuring that neither France, to the 1860s, nor Germany thereafter would gain a predominant influence in the Lowlands and thereby alter the balance of power. In these cases, although the technical aspects of neutralization did not change in the century after 1815, its political significance did, fluctuating with every shift in the balance of power within the European political system of states.

Similarly, in the case of states neutralized since the Second World War, political considerations have loomed large. The neutralization of Austria, in form a self-neutralization without international guarantees, but in fact a maneuver closely related to Soviet policy, was a compromise arrangement. From the Soviet point of view, Austria received independence but remained bound, as it had been under quadripartite occupation, to abstain from international commitments. From the American, British, and French points of view, Austria was freed from partial occupation by Soviet troops. With the achievement of Austrian independence, a strain soon developed between the main concern of Austrian foreign policy, which was to participate in the movement toward the economic integration of Europe through association with the European Economic Community, and the obligation of neutralization as interpreted by Soviet policy. This is a classic example of the distinction between the technical and political aspects of neutralization.

In the case of the neutralization of Laos in 1962, the

primary aim appears to have been to avoid a conflict between the major states in a region that was not of immediate concern to their security. In this instance, neutralization has served the purpose of effecting a hands-off policy in regard to Laos on the part of the larger states, while allowing smaller neighboring states that also served as guarantors to intervene in Laotian affairs on a limited basis.

In the hypothetical case of the neutralization of South Vietnam, the political consequences would depend on the circumstances under which neutralization was achieved. Neutralization might be agreed to following the establishment of full control over the country by the South Vietnamese government with American and other foreign assistance; or under circumstances in which neither of the two contending groups of forces had gained a clear-cut advantage; or after a victory on the part of the National Liberation Front with the assistance of North Vietnam and its allies. The formal conditions of neutralization might be very similar under these three alternatives, but the political consequences would vary significantly. Neutralization, like peace, is a vessel that can hold a wide variety of contents.

THE INTERNATIONAL ROLE OF STATES

The importance of the political consequences of neutralization lies in the fact that the international system assumes the participation of all member states on an equal basis for most purposes. To the extent that individual states are removed from the international system as a result of neutralization, that system is altered. An extensive use of neutralization of states as a solution to controversies between major states would involve a fundamental reorganization of the international system.

At present the international system may be said to operate on two levels: the formal level represented by the United Nations and the institutions associated with it; and the informal level of collective defense arrangements, blocs, and alliances. Under the Charter of the United Nations all member states are pledged to refrain from aggression against other states and to take action against aggressors as decided by the Security Council in accordance with Article 43. Consequently, it may be maintained either that under this system of security neutralization is not necessary, insofar as the security of all states is already provided for, or that neutralization tends to undermine the security provisions of the Charter by introducing redundant procedures that weaken and interfere with those established under the Charter. Indeed, the Charter does not make reference to neutralization, and its provisions are based on the presupposition that all member states are equally capable in terms of their international commitments of participating in such security measures as may be called for by membership in the United Nations. The argument in favor of the admission of neutralized states into the United Nations assumes, not that they would receive an exceptional status, but that the provisions of the Charter in regard to security are so flexible that states with a neutralized status would not be called upon to violate their obligations as neutrals.

At the informal level of collective defense arrangements and other groupings, neutralization plays a much more significant role. Neutralized states are explicitly enjoined from participating in military or political alliances and blocs, and the question of their participation in regional economic groupings is a matter of continuing controversy insofar as such groupings may entail political consequences. A state that is neutralized is, if originally nonaligned, no longer available for membership in an alliance system or, if originally a member of such a group, required to withdraw from it. In the former case, the status quo would be maintained in the informal balance between political groupings; in the latter case, the status quo would be altered by a shift in the balance of power. If this latter case were generalized and a number of states that were members of political groupings were neutralized, a major change in the international system might result.

The political consequences of neutralization would thus appear to be more far-reaching at the informal than at the formal level of the international system. The political implications of the withdrawal of a state from a grouping by virtue of its neutralization derive not only from the consequent reduction in the membership of that grouping but also from the increased ability of one grouping to impose its will on another. The neutralization of a member of the United Nations, on the other hand, is not likely to be so disruptive. One can doubtless imagine circumstances in which decisions of the Security Council under Article 43 might be affected by the limitations placed on certain member states by virtue of their neutralization, but this appears to be the only important way that neutralization might disturb the formal machinery of the United Nations.

Still, though these formal and informal levels of the international system are distinct, they are not separate. Indeed, the debates and voting in the General Assembly and the Security Council usually reflect in some detail the political relationships that exist at the informal level. In this sense, then, international politics as represented by the decisions of the United Nations is as likely to be affected by the neutralization of states as is the informal level of the international system.

The political significance to the international system of the neutralization of states may be envisaged by considering the situations that would be created by a widespread use of neutralization. Varying degrees of nonalignment, neutralism, and demilitarization have been proposed for many groups of countries in Central Europe, the Middle East, Asia, Africa, and Latin America. It would not be difficult to imagine the extension to these countries of formal neutralization guaranteed by the major states, presumably the permanent members of the Security Council. The effect of such a development would be an international system in which the major states concentrated all the decisionmaking power in their hands and the large number of neutralized states committed themselves to abstaining from all military and political alliances. In the United Nations this solution would lead to the domination of the Security Council over the General Assembly and, within the Security Council, to the domination of the nonpermanent members by the permanent to a much greater extent than at present.

The establishment of this kind of system would scarcely be possible without agreement among the major states, but there is no assurance that they would remain in agreement for a long period of time. It would tend to make the international system more rigid in that change would depend increasingly on unanimity among the permanent members of the Security Council. More particularly, the neutralization of large states (Germany, Japan, India, Indonesia) would remove them from peacekeeping roles and would correspondingly increase the burden on the guarantor states. Such a system might well work if it were accepted by all the neutralized states and if there were in fact agreement among the guarantor states on the evolving and ever-changing role of states in the international system, but it is most unlikely that these conditions will be met in the world as we know it. An international system involving a widespread use of neutralization would thus depend largely on the relations among the guarantor states, and for the foreseeable future these will probably not be any more congenial than they have been in the past decade.

At the other end of the scale, one may envisage a situation in which no states are neutralized. This is, in fact, the assumption on which the Charter of the United Nations is based, and it would imply an international system maintained by the procedures provided for in the Charter. An international system without neutralized states would not necessarily be one in which demilitarized or "atom-free" states or groups of states could not be established. The control, or the limitation of the dissemination, of nuclear and other weapons is a separate and distinct issue from that of the neutralization of states. Separate also is the question of national policies of non-alignment which do not involve commitments or formal recognition by other states and do not affect the peace-keeping machinery of the United Nations. Similarly, such a system would not affect the neutralization of parts of states, territories, canals, rivers, and other regions that are not states.

CHAPTER IV

AREAS SUITABLE FOR NEUTRALIZATION

NEUTRALIZATION is relevant primarily to geographically definable areas in which two or more external actors have substantial and competitive interests. There are, therefore, several categories of conflict to which the notion of neutralization is largely irrelevant. At one extreme, there is little role for neutralization arrangements in internal upheavals accompanied by no external interference. In such cases there is nothing from which to neutralize the conflict. Neutralization also seems irrelevant when direct conflict between sovereign states involves no intermediate territory or geographical entity. Here there is, in effect, nothing that can be neutralized.

Many conflicts in contemporary international politics, however, do not fall into either of these pure types. External parties do intervene competitively in the affairs of states or territories already undergoing severe internal disintegration, upheaval, and civil strife—as in Vietnam, Cyprus, and Yemen. From the perspective of world order, the desirability of neutralization seems particularly great in such situations even though the feasibility of neutralization may be undermined by some of the same factors that make it seem desirable. In addition, external actors sometimes intervene competitively in the affairs of states that have some real capacity for self-government and are not so disrupted by civil strife as to make self-regulation impossible—as in Austria prior to the State Treaty of 1955. The feasibility of neutralization is apt to be greater in such cases since internal viability tends to reduce both the opportunities and the temptations for outside actors to resume their interventions.

Three Approaches to the Question of Suitability

There are several perspectives from which it is possible to approach the problem of delineating areas suitable for neutralization.

FUNCTIONS OF NEUTRALIZATION

Perhaps the most commonly cited functions of neutralization deal with the reduction and regulation of overt hostilities. Neutralization may be employed to prevent the outbreak of a violent clash in an area already subjected to the intrusion of competitive political interests of outside actors. In such cases neutralization would operate as an anticipatory, rather than an *ex post facto,* device. Neutralization may also be utilized to help terminate overt hostilities, supported by external interventions, in which neither side can hope to gain a decisive advantage at the existing level of conflict and in which the principal parties fear the consequences of uncontrolled escalation. In addition, there is the possibility of an intermediate role for neutralization focusing on the notion of moderating a conflict even though it may not be possible to terminate it entirely. But, insofar as neutralization operates in this way, it is likely to emerge only from a partially successful attempt at prevention or termination.

There are other functions that neutralization can perform, too. Arrangements resembling neutralization have been discussed as devices for accomplishing the reunification of divided states such as Germany and Korea. Insofar as such divisions are perpetuated by the impact of competitive political alignments, neutralization—since it offers an outcome in which neither side would necessarily gain at the expense of the other—offers interesting possibilities for solutions. Finally, neutralization may function simply to remove a geographical area or object of value from the realm of political competition in the international arena. As such, a neutralization arrangement constitutes an agreement among the relevant contestants to carry on their competition elsewhere. This notion of removal from contention has generally been applied to small states, but it seems equally relevant to various non-state regions, such as outer space or the Antarctic.

POTENTIAL SUBJECTS OF NEUTRALIZATION

What types of area should be treated as candidates for neutralization? The most important candidates are states. Perhaps the most commonly suggested subjects of neutralization in the current era are, first, emergent and internally weak states (such as Laos) and, second, divided states (such as Germany and Vietnam). The problems generated by these states are particularly vexing in contemporary international politics. And both types of state constitute characteristic focuses of competitive intervention by outside powers. Although these factors make the notion of neutralization attractive in such cases, they also tend to generate serious obstacles to the achievement and success of neutralization.

Several other types of area can be regarded as potential candidates for neutralization. It may seem desirable to neutralize geographical regions, such as Southeast Asia, that are nominally composed of several sovereign states. Such a possibility would be especially important when the patterns of external intervention

68

sharply curtail the prospects of stabilizing the internal politics of any one of the states without regulating the instabilities of the whole region. Next, the international arena presently contains a number of keenly disputed territories that have no claim to sovereignty in themselves and that might be made subjects of neutralization both to regulate the conflict of the external claimants and to offer the people involved some sense of self-determination. Kashmir and the Gaza Strip illustrate these problems. A variation on this pattern occasionally arises when an important city becomes a major focus of conflict between two competing states. The idea of neutralizing or internationalizing cities has arisen in recent years in connection with Jerusalem, Trieste, and Berlin. Finally, there are various service facilities and resources in the world that have no claim to independent sovereignty and that might be subjected to neutralization to remove them from the realm of interstate competition. Several of the major international canals and the Antarctic, for example, might fall into this category.

POLITICAL FEASIBILITY OF NEUTRALIZATION

It is important to consider first whether the decision-makers of the potential subject genuinely desire neutralization, whether they are ready to accept the full implications of such an arrangement for the international status of the subject, and, in any case, whether they are capable of performing the obligations embodied in the arrangement. Such questions are, of course, fully relevant only when the potential subject of neutralization possesses genuine sovereignty or some real independence. Beyond this, there are numerous questions concerning the advantages and drawbacks of a given neutralization arrangement for the relevant external actors.

And this set of problems is apt to be particularly complex in concrete cases. In addition, the feasibility of neutralization is generally dependent on the *de facto* effects of such an arrangement on existing patterns of international politics. In short, neutralization may well imply a number of changes in the postures and activities of the actors involved beyond those specifically outlined in the agreement that may be only dimly perceived at the outset.

Reunification Through Neutralization—Germany

The division of Germany has become one of the most influential and intractable problems of postwar international politics. Although neutralization has never been formally debated as a means of reunifying Germany, it is a significant possibility given the important links between Germany's geopolitical situation and the broader strategic balance, and it has been informally suggested from time to time in the debates over such concepts as disengagement.[1] Nevertheless, the obstacles to German neutralization appear decisive at the present time.

There is no doubt that most Germans desire to see their country reunified. The effective strength of this desire, however, is far from clear. What priority do the Germans attach to reunification and what price are they willing to pay in political terms to achieve it? Neither the Federal Republic of Germany (FRG) nor the German Democratic Republic (GDR) presently seems willing to buy reunification at the cost of its own political

[1] For additional material on this idea, see Coral Bell, *Negotiation from Strength* (New York 1963), especially Chap. 7, and Richard J. Barnet and Marcus Raskin, *After 20 Years: Alternatives to the Cold War in Europe* (New York 1965), Chap. IV.

identity or any significant portion thereof. In the absence of gross coercion, neither Germany is willing to be assimilated into the sociopolitical structure of the other. Moreover, neither side is willing to give serious consideration to some mixed form of government because both are doubtful that it would prove viable and because both fear that a nonviable coalition would ultimately be asymmetrical and detrimental. The fear of negative long-term results makes each side so suspicious of proposals for attaining political unification offered by the other side that all initiatives are doomed to failure from the start.

There are, in addition, more specific ambivalences in the attitudes of both West Germans and East Germans. Although the West Germans appear to have a particularly strong commitment to reunification, their spectacular postwar recovery and material prosperity have tended to immerse them in their own affairs, to make them eager to avoid moves that might jeopardize their gains, and to generate concern over the possibility that the addition of East Germany might at first produce a "spread" effect in terms of economic prosperity.[2] The West German elite, also, appears to hesitate over the potential effects of reunification on the country's party structure as well as the possibility of Communist subversion and attempts at takeover of some compromise form of government. From their clear-cut minority position, the East Germans evidently fear that reunification might mean a *de facto* submersion of the GDR resulting in the loss of the political and social principles for which they stand. Moreover, recent indications that the East

---

[2] The economic "spread" effect, however, may be a factor of declining importance because of the GDR's increased economic vitality during the 1960s.

German government is having some success in fostering East German loyalties and perspectives suggest that the salience and urgency of reunification may be declining in the East. This conclusion is further supported by the marked economic advances of the GDR since the Berlin crisis of 1961.

At the same time, the extent to which the major external powers have a genuine desire to see Germany reunified seems limited. The Soviets now openly indicate that they would prefer formal acceptance of a permanent division of Germany to reunification on any terms other than their own. They have advocated a formalization of the split since the fall of 1958.[3] Behind this posture lies what appears to be a genuine fear of a united Germany as a threat to Soviet security interests and a real concern that a united Germany, as the most powerful state on the continent, would become a major political competitor in areas of interest to the Soviet Union. Thus, strong Soviet efforts to maintain the GDR as the formal bastion of Soviet security in Europe continue,[4] and there is evident apprehension in connection with the rapidly changing political map of Eastern Europe. Soviet reluctance is heightened by similar pressures from Eastern European states, such as Poland and

[3] During the early years of the postwar period the Soviets advocated reunification of Germany. In fact, Soviet leaders appear to have been willing to contemplate the idea of a neutral Germany on several occasions. With the growing strength of the FRG, however, the Soviets have shifted more and more to advocacy of a formal and permanent division of Germany. They undoubtedly fear that German reunification would lead to dominance by the FRG.

[4] The Group of Soviet Forces in Germany (GSFG), for example, still contains twenty Soviet divisions. In addition, the six divisions of the GDR are evidently under the command of the GSFG. For further details, consult *The Military Balance, 1967–1968* (London 1967).

Czechoslovakia, which tend to view a united Germany as a threat to their own security.

Although the Western powers have explicitly endorsed the goal of German reunification and although the FRG was incorporated into NATO at least partially on the basis of this posture, there are still ambivalences in Western attitudes toward German reunification, perhaps most evidently in the case of France, the principal alternative to Germany for the role of most influential political force on the continent. A united Germany would be substantially larger than France in terms of population, industrial capacity, overall economy, and military potential. In addition, Germany's strategic geopolitical position would tend to heighten its influence in Europe, while its dynamic economic posture might make it more appealing to other countries than France as an economic partner.

The United States and Britain also have cause for concern at the prospect of a united Germany. While the United States has been perhaps the most consistent external advocate of German reunification, American decisionmakers have always admitted, under questioning, to a sense of trepidation about the probable political posture of a united Germany and to a residual fear that Germany might again endanger international peace and security. More concretely, the deep-seated American concern with the overall strategic balance between East and West, coupled with various geopolitical consequences of a reunification of Germany through disengagement or neutralization, has produced strong negative reactions in the United States to proposals along these lines. The United States has tended to emphasize that a reunification of Germany along these lines would

73

constitute a decisive blow to the NATO alliance, produce asymmetry in the international system, and weaken the West in the overall strategic balance.[5] Under the circumstances, the real meaning of the verbal support for German reunification of even the most favorable external power is anything but unambiguous and unreserved.

German neutralization would almost certainly necessitate some major changes in current and emerging patterns of international politics which various states would be reluctant to accept. A united and neutralized Germany would probably have to withdraw from both security pacts and the economic arrangements to which the FRG and the GDR presently belong. This withdrawal would, in effect, mean the end of the NATO and Warsaw Pact alliances as they are presently constituted, a result that might produce disturbing uncertainties in European security owing to its perceived asymmetrical impact on the East-West relationship. Perhaps even more important politically is the fact that German neutralization would require a withdrawal from GDR membership in the Comecon and FRG membership in the Common

[5] The most frequently mentioned problem in this area concerns conventional force levels. Whereas the reunification of Germany through neutralization would presumably necessitate the withdrawal of substantial American conventional strength from the continent, it would only require a withdrawal of Warsaw Pact forces into Eastern Europe. A number of current developments, however, appear to be mitigating these fears of asymmetrical consequences at the conventional level. These developments include: rapid improvements in Western airlift capabilities; a decline in the perceived importance of the Soviet threat; growing political objections to the maintenance of American conventional forces on the continent; the preoccupation of the United States with other parts of the world; and changing relationships between the states of Eastern Europe and the Soviet Union.

Market and other organizations of Western European unity as they are presently constituted. Such withdrawals would retard current movements toward integration in both halves of Europe. This is not to say that alternative and more inclusive arrangements for European integration would not ultimately emerge. Such a sharp disruption of current patterns of European politics would inevitably, however, be met by strong political opposition and would come up against the rigidities imposed by existing patterns of commitments and institutions.

From a longer-term perspective, the reunification of Germany through neutralization could have profound effects on international politics. A more inclusive, though somewhat looser, pattern of European integration might emerge. The superpowers might engage in greater efforts at coordination to deal with the problems developing from new patterns of politics on the continent. Or, again, the new Germany might become an increasingly nationalistic force, either as France is in the current period or in some more overt and insistent form. In short, a wide range of new and far-reaching developments would become plausible. Insofar as German reunification were successful, however, the new Germany would almost certainly emerge as the most powerful force in Central Europe and, therefore, as the key to the future of the continent. This would be the case even if substantial limitations of a formal nature were placed on the ability and freedom of Germany to participate in international politics.[6] These far-reaching implications of reunification would almost certainly catalyze doubts

[6] For example, it would be possible in formal terms to restrict Germany's overall military strength (as was done at Versailles in 1919) or to demand that Germany remain a nonnuclear state (as was done for the FRG in the Accords of Paris in 1954).

and objections to the reunification of Germany through neutralization at the present time.

Perhaps the most important conclusion to be drawn from this discussion is that Germany is simply too important to be neutralized. Neutralization may work for small states whose neutralization would not seriously alter or disrupt existing patterns of international politics.[7] But the neutralization of a major state—rather than being simply an *ad hoc* solution to a particular problem which leaves the international arena itself essentially unchanged—is apt to involve fundamental changes in international politics.

Preventing Competitive Intervention— The Gaza Strip

The most fundamental difficulty in utilizing neutralization to prevent competitive and forceful intervention by external powers in a contentious area is that it requires *prior* identification and action. But the situation may not be regarded as particularly important prior to intervention by external powers. It is often difficult to generate a sense of urgency about a situation before the actual occurrence of dangerous developments. In addition, potential intervenors may be unwilling to relinquish the prospects of gain from future interventions in a given area on an *ex ante* basis.

From the perspective of preventive neutralization, the Gaza Strip, a small piece of territory lying between the Sinai Desert and the Mediterranean Sea and inhabited primarily by Palestinian refugees, is of con-

[7] It is at least conceivable that Korea could be placed in this category.

siderable interest. From 1957 to 1967 the Strip was, for all practical purposes, a neutralized area even though it was nominally under the administration of the United Arab Republic (UAR).[8] This was made possible through the physical deployment of the United Nations Emergency Force (UNEF) in the area and the continuing involvement of the United Nations in the fate of the refugee population of the Gaza Strip.[9] The relative success of this arrangement for the Gaza Strip during the decade of its existence indicates the potential value of neutralizing such non-sovereign areas. Several other aspects of this case also deserve emphasis, however, in the present discussion. Although the *de facto* neutralization of the Gaza Strip served a preventive function from 1957 onward, the arrangement was only achieved in the aftermath of major hostilities which made possible actions that otherwise would almost certainly have been politically unfeasible. Moreover, these arrangements for the Gaza Strip proved incapable of surviving further hostilities of major proportions between Israel and the UAR during 1967. While it is possible that the Strip will be reneutralized in the future, therefore, it would be a mistake to suppose that such a move would be likely to have a far-reaching impact on the broader Arab-Israeli conflict.

A major factor that facilitated the *de facto* neutralization of the Gaza Strip from 1957 to 1967 was the fact

[8] For material on the processes through which this arrangement came into existence in the aftermath of the crisis of October and November 1956, see Gabriella Rosner, *The United Nations Emergency Force* (New York 1963).

[9] For further material on these arrangements, see Hamilton Fish Armstrong, "U.N. Experience in Gaza," *Foreign Affairs*, XXXV, July 1957, 600–619.

that the area had no collective political will of its own.[10] The internal political situation of the subject area, therefore, was not an important barrier to neutralization. Several other local factors also helped to make neutralization a feasible arrangement for the Strip. The territory is small enough so that it could be effectively isolated from Israel and the UAR by the UNEF contingents. As a result, it was difficult for either of these states to violate the arrangement, even on an indirect basis, except in a highly visible fashion. In addition, the stationing of UNEF contingents along the international boundary line between Israel and the UAR from the Gaza Strip to the Gulf of Aqaba reduced the opportunities for low level and sporadic acts of a disturbing nature that might have undermined the *de facto* neutralization.

Perhaps the most critical factor in the success of the neutralization of the Gaza Strip, however, was the tacit acquiescence of Israel and the UAR, the external parties that had previously made the area an object of dangerous contention. Even before the 1967 crisis, the fact that the Arab-Israeli dispute remained very much alive meant that the viability of the arrangements for the Gaza Strip could never simply be taken for granted. There were, nevertheless, several factors that exerted pressure in support of the arrangement during the 1957–1967 period. First, the alternatives did not seem desirable for either side. For Israel, *de facto* neutralization constituted the only real alternative to outright UAR control of the Strip or offensive military operations that seemed likely to produce substantial negative consequences for Israel.

---

[10] The Gaza Strip was used from time to time as a base for Arab commandos and for the organizational activities of the Palestine Liberation Army (PLA). There was, however, never any question of sovereignty or political independence for the Strip itself.

For the UAR, the arrangement represented the major alternative to sharply increased prospects of a large-scale Israeli attack on UAR territory. And the continued existence of the unsettled refugees in the Gaza Strip was of some value to the Egyptians in maintaining their position of leadership in the Arab-Israeli dispute. Second, since the *de facto* neutralization arrangement was always designated as temporary and nonpermanent, both sides could rationalize acquiescence on an *ad hoc* basis and avoid pressures to reach some more permanent solution. Third, there were significant pressures on both sides from powers outside the region—especially the United States and Britain—to continue to accept the arrangement. These pressures were widely believed to include the prospect of support for any local power that became a victim of aggression, as well as more negative sanctions. Fourth, serious disturbances of the arrangements existing in the area between 1957 and 1967 were likely to result in the destruction of the United Nations presence. And despite the legal ambiguities of UNEF's position in the area,[11] neither Israel nor the UAR could hope to remove the Force without generating serious negative international reactions.

Even though the *de facto* neutralization of the Gaza Strip did not require fundamental changes in the incentives of the various actors in the area, it did have important consequences for the patterns of international politics in the Middle East. In a sense, the arrangement constituted a partial bar to Egyptian hegemony in the Arab area. One of the most effective ways for the UAR

[11] On this subject, see Rosner, *op. cit.,* Chap. III, as well as the "Report of the Secretary-General on the Withdrawal of the United Nations Emergency Force (UNEF)," *UN Monthly Chronicle,* IV, no. 7 (July 1967), 135–170.

to extend its influence among the Arab states is to move toward more active prosecution of the conflict with Israel. Insofar as the Gaza Strip arrangement put limits on subsequent UAR-Israel confrontations, therefore, it also tended to inhibit the leadership role of the Egyptians within the Arab movement. Beyond this, the Gaza Strip arrangement tended to freeze international relationships in the Middle East and thereby prevent more far-reaching changes that might ultimately have produced new and more viable patterns of international politics in the area. The problem here, of course, was that more far-reaching changes would undoubtedly have produced substantial violence on a local scale and might well have embroiled the great powers in dangerous undertakings before a more viable pattern of relationships emerged. Nevertheless, the freezing effects of the *de facto* neutralization of the Gaza Strip between 1957 and 1967 marked it as a temporary, though valuable, expedient rather than as a satisfactory longer-term solution.

Terminating Competitive Intervention—
South Vietnam

For neutralization to be relevant to the termination of overt hostilities in areas experiencing extensive intervention by several outside states, there are two basic prerequisites. The conflict must be perceived by the major participants to be approaching a stalemate, but they must continue to demonstrate resolve as well as physical strength with regard to the situation. If the participants do not see a stalemate arising,[12] at least

---

[12] Stalemate, in the formal sense of neither side being able to make any move without losing, is not required. If both sides become convinced that it is impossible to win in any meaningful sense

some will continue to seek outright victory without interminable delays or inordinate costs. On the other hand, sharp asymmetries with regard to resolve are likely to be a prelude to physical developments sufficiently decisive to make the notion of neutralization irrelevant. In the present conflict in South Vietnam these basic prerequisites may exist or may come to exist. But the conflict illustrates the complexities and ambiguities that underlie these basic prerequisites.[13]

The fact that South Vietnam itself is in a state of fundamental political and social disruption casts doubt on the feasibility of a neutralization arrangement. Both the regime in Saigon and the National Liberation Front (NLF) are under the influence of their respective outside supporters to a considerable, though not very measurable, degree. They are not, therefore, entirely free agents in developing attitudes toward the prospect of neutralization. Moreover, it is by no means clear, in any case, whether the Saigon regime and the NLF would regard neutralization as an attractive prospect and therefore cooperate willingly in such an arrangement. Above all, it is anything but clear what group or coalition would come out on top in political terms following the withdrawal of external forces from South Vietnam.[14] It is probable that there would be a continuation of civil strife for some time. And the ultimate victors might be

without engaging in a protracted, costly, and indeterminate conflict, a rough condition of stalemate exists.

[13] The case of the Yemen also provides illustrations of these problems at the present time.

[14] It is also important to note that various forms and degrees of withdrawal on the part of external powers are possible. A failure on the part of one or more parties to withdraw entirely, especially if the failure was sharply asymmetrical, would have important effects on the internal political balances.

difficult to recognize in terms of the present composition of either the Saigon regime or the NLF. It is also difficult to gauge the sentiments on the question of neutralization of the various social and ethnic groups within South Vietnam which are at present largely unrepresented by either the Saigon regime or the Liberation Front. Finally, the very absence of a viable political structure in South Vietnam would itself generate serious problems for a neutralization arrangement regardless of stated desires. New internal disturbances would be apt to raise incentives for intervention from outside states, to generate opportunities for intervention, and to offer a situation in which various forms of indirect intervention could be undertaken with a low level of visibility.

Nevertheless, the internal situation of South Vietnam is not wholly unamenable to a solution based on neutralization. The very fact that neutralization would not require a decisive or immediate settlement of the internal political conflicts of South Vietnam could conceivably appeal to all the major factions within the country. In effect, neutralization would provide a somewhat less dangerous format for the continuation of the indigenous struggle.[15] Moreover, the likelihood of renewed intervention by external powers would depend on other factors in addition to the internal situation in South Vietnam. Such factors would include the exact nature of the initial withdrawals, the perceived costs to the external powers of a policy of reintervention, and the nature of the control machinery set up to assist in the maintenance of the neutralization arrangement.

[15] Neutralization does not in any way preclude a continuation of indigenous strife. In South Vietnam it would not even preclude eventual unification with the North so long as unification did not result from coercion on the part of the DRV.

Perhaps the most important factor in assessing the feasibility of terminating external intervention in South Vietnam through neutralization, however, is the willingness of the relevant external powers to agree to such an arrangement. It is unclear whether the postures of the two most important states, the United States and the Democratic Republic of Vietnam (DRV), can be brought into line with the twin conditions of perceived stalemate and continued resolve. In addition to the fact that neither external power has anything like complete control over its internal ally,[16] several important factors diminish their sympathy for such a settlement. There are continuing hopes for major asymmetrical gains; almost day-to-day fluctuations in the evaluations of the major parties with regard to critical issues; and the weight of felt commitments to victory arising from ideological considerations and past expenditures of physical and human resources on the Vietnam war.

But there are also important factors in the Vietnam situation pushing the major external powers toward the basic prerequisites for neutralization. And the very continuation of major hostilities appears to heighten the salience of several of these factors. First, there is little indication that either of the major intervenors is willing to allow a decisively and obviously asymmetrical conclusion of the war so long as there are escalatory options at hand—as is evident at the present time. For this reason, a kind of contingent stalemate may emerge in South Vietnam even though the proximate balances of strength

---

[16] It is extremely difficult to pin down relationships of this kind with any precision. In South Vietnam, however, the fact that the United States and the DRV have become symbolically committed to their local clients gives both the Saigon regime and the NLF substantial power over the policies of the external powers.

on the ground continue to fluctuate considerably on a day-to-day basis. Second, and related to the first point, a continuation or escalation of the hostilities in South Vietnam will tend to heighten the already substantial fears that highly dangerous and perhaps uncontrollable escalatory sequences could be touched off by the Vietnam war. It is probable that the various external powers are differentially susceptible to this fear. The United States and the Soviet Union, as the powers with the most destructive military capabilities and the most to lose from military destruction, are no doubt the most susceptible. Nevertheless, the DRV and China can scarcely ignore the prospect. Third, in terms of purely economic costs the war is now producing serious incentives within the various external powers to call a halt. Moreover, when this problem is viewed from the perspective of opportunity costs and when human and political costs are added to direct economic costs, these disadvantages of continuing the war become a major factor. The influence of this factor is also no doubt asymmetrical. Among the external powers, the costs of the war would appear to be greatest to the United States and the DRV. Moreover, given the present state of the conflict, the war may appear to the Chinese as a relatively cheap way to tie up American resources, to weaken the American will to participate in such messy local situations in the future, and to discredit American foreign policy in world opinion. Fourth, it is possible that a neutralization arrangement could be set up for South Vietnam without the participation of all the potentially relevant external powers. There may well be some incentives among the external powers to agree to the neutralization of South Vietnam as a means of affecting the future balance of power in Southeast Asia. Although it is clear that neutralization could not succeed without the consent of the United States and the DRV, it is not clear that the consent of China would be required. In this connection, it is at least conceivable that the neutralization of South Vietnam could result from a United States-DRV-Soviet Union agreement based on a desire to create a barrier to future Chinese expansion in Southeast Asia and a consequent concern to develop a more viable balance of power in the area.

An agreement to terminate outside intervention in South Vietnam through a neutralization arrangement would also raise some important questions concerning existing and emerging patterns of international politics in the area. Interestingly, neutralization of South Vietnam would not require drastic changes in the present formal organizational arrangements.[17] It would not even necessarily raise the question of the compatibility of a neutralized status with United Nations membership since South Vietnam is not at present a member of the organization.[18]

Beyond this, however, there are several major links between such a neutralization arrangement and surrounding patterns of international politics. First, the problems of redeploying the military forces of the relevant external powers might generate serious difficulties. It would, for example, be an extensive and time-consuming task for the United States to withdraw its forces from South Vietnam. Moreover, a number of problems would arise if the relevant external powers were also

[17] South Vietnam does not belong to any multilateral security arrangements. The only formal change required would be an abrogation of the security commitments between the United States and the Republic of Vietnam.

[18] For a discussion of the problem of United Nations membership for neutralized states, see *supra,* Chap. III, 51ff.

required to withdraw their forces from certain neighboring areas, such as Thailand and Laos. Provisions of this kind would be difficult to enforce. And they would raise the problem of asymmetrical effects on the interests of the various powers since American decisionmakers would probably perceive such an arrangement as placing greater limitations on the United States than on the DRV in the event of a subsequent breakdown of the neutralization arrangement for South Vietnam.[19] Second, given the existing political structure of Indochina, the problems of local political nonviability and indirect aggression might seriously undermine the possibilities of maintaining a neutralization arrangement in South Vietnam. In short. it is far from clear that neutralization can be maintained in an isolated area that is surrounded by other states of doubtful internal viability which might serve as springboards for clandestine intervention in the neutralized area. Third, even if it could be made viable, neutralization might generate serious problems for South Vietnam in acquiring the massive economic assistance it would clearly need. As long as the internal political struggle was still going on in the area, it would be difficult to establish the limits of legitimate assistance to any one of the competing sets of authorities within South Vietnam. And, in any case, assistance emanating from any outside party would always be subject to the charge that it prejudiced the political situation within

[19] It is quite possible that American decisionmakers overestimate this problem. With regard to the problem of indirect violations, the United States may well be at a disadvantage. Whether the United States would find it harder than the DRV to resume a major role in South Vietnam in the event of a breakdown of neutralization, however, is open to question. For some interesting comments on this problem, see Albert Wohlstetter, "Illusions of Distance," *Foreign Affairs,* XLVI, no. 2 (January 1968), 242–255.

the country. If, however, the internal situation were to stabilize, it is conceivable that this problem of economic assistance could be handled by channeling all aid for South Vietnam through international agencies or some form of international consortium encompassing all the relevant outside parties.

Modifying Competitive Intervention—Laos

Neutralization may also function to modify the levels and effects of competitive intervention by outside powers without terminating the intervention altogether. It is unlikely, however, that a neutralization arrangement could be deliberately negotiated with this intermediate objective in mind. Both prevention and termination are conceptually clear-cut since they incorporate an either/or view of intervention. The notion of modification, on the other hand, involves ambiguous distinctions and raises extraordinarily difficult problems of definition. For this reason, it would be difficult to negotiate an agreement along these lines deliberately, especially in a situation characterized by ongoing intervention of indefinite proportions. Modification of competitive intervention, however, might well be the actual result of an only partially successful neutralization agreement originally negotiated for purposes of prevention or termination, because the consequences of violation are seldom an either/or matter. It is quite possible for the participants to continue to view a neutralization agreement as advantageous in overall terms even though significant violations occur. In this connection, the critical distinction concerns the threshold level below which violations, while significant, are not so important as to disrupt the arrangement entirely.

87

The case of Laos constitutes an excellent illustration of these conclusions. Laos was formally neutralized by the Geneva agreement of 1962, an agreement designed to terminate the substantial interventions that were occurring at the time.[20] Although the agreement contains relatively extensive control provisions, it was never fully implemented and it has since been violated by the renewal of outside interventions from several sources. Nevertheless, the 1962 agreement has, on balance, had a noticeable effect on subsequent developments in Laos, and the principal external powers continue to view it as having some value.[21]

A number of factors operating simultaneously have produced the peculiarly mixed outcome of neutralization in Laos. Two factors stand out among those that have limited the success of the arrangement. The elites of the country did not succeed in developing a viable national government in the aftermath of the 1962 agreement. During late 1962 and 1963 hostilities were renewed on a substantial scale between the contending factions, and the country has since been effectively partitioned on a geographical basis for purposes of government. External powers are therefore able to intervene with relative ease in those parts of the state controlled by factions they support. In addition, the development of the Vietnam war has tended to encourage certain types of intervention in Laos. There are incentives to

[20] For a good discussion of the circumstances in which this agreement was negotiated, as well as the text of the agreement, consult George Modelski, "International Conference on the Settlement of the Laotian Question, 1961–1962" (Canberra 1962).

[21] For further material on this point, see our "Neutralization in Southeast Asia: Problems and Prospects," A Study Prepared at the Request of the Committee on Foreign Relations, United States Senate (Washington, D.C., October 10, 1966), Appendix C.

utilize Laotian territory for supply operations, and various units make use of Laotian territory as a sanctuary. These activities naturally raise the incentives for counter-interventions. Moreover, the cover provided by the concurrence of a major war in Vietnam tends to make it easier for outsiders to intervene in Laos without attracting a great deal of attention.

There are also several factors in the Laotian situation which have prevented the neutralization arrangement from becoming entirely meaningless. First, the effective physical partition of the country means that external interventions restricted to either part of it are unlikely to determine decisively the future of the whole country. The relative clarity of the partition tends to operate as a barrier to any spreading of the influence of external intervention even though it facilitates intervention *within* various segments of the country. Second, both the United States and the Soviet Union, while they have continued to show some interest in limited interventions in Laos, have complementary interests in postures of restraint in the area. These interests are based on the desire to avoid extensive commitments in a messy local situation, to minimize the escalatory potential of extensive mutual interventions in Laos, to cooperate to preclude the expansion of Chinese influence in the area, and to continue policies based on Soviet-American detente in various other areas.[22] Third, although the war in Vietnam has generated significant opportunities for outside intervention in Laos, it has also produced a desire to hold Laos in abeyance while the action in Vietnam is unfolding. In

[22] For a more extensive discussion of Soviet-American interests along these lines, see Oran R. Young, "Political Discontinuities in the International System," *World Politics*, XX, no. 3 (April 1968), 369–392.

short, neither side seems prepared to see the Vietnam war, at its present level of violence, spread to the whole of Indochina. Fourth, the existence of the international control machinery, together with the international attention devoted to events in Laos, sometimes operates in support of this pattern of limited restraints. Although this factor certainly should not be overemphasized, the fact that there is a relatively high level of concern in the international community with developments in Laos does tend to inhibit at least some of the most obvious types of external intervention in the country.

Removal from Contention—Space

Another function of neutralization involves an agreement on the part of states with extended competitive interests simply to define another state or object of interest as outside the boundaries of their competitive relations. The purpose of neutralization in such circumstances is to delimit the scope of competitive relations without materially affecting the nature of the ongoing competition over other matters. This conception of neutralization is similar to the nineteenth-century practice of removing certain small states such as Belgium from the realm of great power interactions.[23] In the contemporary era removal from contention through neutralization is relevant to certain nonstate entities such as outer space, Antarctica, and various service facilities. Although the formal language of neutralization has not been used, both the 1959 treaty on Antarctica [24] and the

[23] For a discussion of the Belgian case, see *supra*, Chap. II, 24ff.
[24] For the text of this treaty, see United States Department of State, *The Conference on Antarctica: Conference Documents, The*

1966 treaty on the exploration of outer space [25] provide for arrangements that amount to neutralization.

The space agreement offers particularly clear illustrations of a number of factors that make removal from contention through neutralization an interesting possibility in the contemporary world. The newness of the space arena tends to make it a desirable candidate for neutralization. There is, for example, no long history of disputes, competing commitments, vested interests, and rigid postures affecting the disposition of space. In addition, space is an excellent example of an area of considerable importance which is relatively separable from the principal arenas of international politics. This separability arises from the relative ease of making a geographical distinction between outer space and the other arenas of international politics, the fact that only the superpowers are presently involved (on any significant scale) in the exploration of space, and the salience of the distincton in international opinion. Separability is also enhanced by the fact that, for most purposes, space can be removed from international contention without materially affecting existing patterns of competition in international politics. Beyond this, the total absence of political will or even a disputed population is a factor substantially reducing the problems of neutralizing space. With regard to maintenance, moreover, the nonexistence of an organized human factor both reduces the scope for violations of the neutralization arrangement and makes violations more evident in the event that they do occur.

Antarctic Treaty, and Related Papers, Department of State Publication No. 7060 (Washington, D.C. 1960).

[25] For the text of this treaty, see the *New York Times,* December 9, 1966, 18.

Conclusion

This discussion is not sufficient to prove anything about the overall importance of neutralization relative to other procedures for the management of power in the contemporary international system. Nevertheless, the problems associated with neutralization should be judged in comparison with the difficulties attendant upon other available procedures for managing power. Insofar as neutralization is regarded as an attractive possibility, it is generally because of its *relative* utility in the specific situation at hand rather than because it represents a panacea or an ideal outcome.

There are some intrinsic limitations on the overall importance of neutralization in international politics. Above all, it is logically impossible to neutralize all states without, in effect, removing the phenomenon of power from international relations, an unlikely occurrence by any standards. To neutralize an entity it is necessary to neutralize it from something. In addition, it is probable that some individual states—such as Germany—are simply too important to be neutralized without qualitative changes in the nature of international politics. While neutralization may be an invaluable device by which to manage certain critical problems, therefore, it is never likely to play more than a supplementary role in the overall processes of managing power in the international system.

CHAPTER V

NEGOTIATING NEUTRALIZATION

NEUTRALIZATION arrangements have typically resulted from sustained and dramatic multilateral negotiations. An examination of the negotiating process will cast some light upon the reasons why states seek to agree to neutralize a country (or other subject of international controversy) and will help to show why such agreements may be difficult to reach or, if reached, may not satisfy the main objectives of some or all of the participants in the negotiations.

Neutralization has generally been advocated as an approach to the management of international conflict. The basic issues in any negotiations aiming at neutralization are accordingly shaped both by the nature of the conflict and by the motivations of the parties in wishing to remove the candidate for neutralization from the arena of active military competition. Sometimes the negotiating situation is one in which neutralization is only one part of a more comprehensive settlement, as was the neutralization of Switzerland and the city of Cracow at the Congress of Vienna; sometimes it is the sole objective of the negotiations, as was the neutralization of Laos in 1962. The distinction is important, since in instances of the former sort neutralization is chosen as one among several coordinated means of bringing stability to international society, whereas in cases of the latter type neutralization is a specific bargain or compromise reached to settle or confine a mutually disadvantageous conflict

93

among the negotiators or, at least, to transform the conflict into less destructive forms.[1]

The goal of this analysis of neutralization negotiations will be to clarify typical bargaining issues and indicate some of the ways in which they have been dealt with in past negotiations. The premise of neutralization negotiations is that the principal parties have both a potential converging interest in establishing a neutralized status for the entity in question and potential or actual diverging motivations and objectives in mind.[2] In the context of negotiations there are two basic sets of relationships: those between the guarantor states *inter se* and those between the guarantor states and the government (and other elite factions) of the state proposed as a candidate for neutralization. If the candidate is a state undergoing civil strife and competitive intervention, then the two sets of relationships may be very intricate. The circumstances conditioning negotiation of neutralization for South Vietnam present a problem of great complexity in this respect. The explication of these patterns will help to indicate when and why neutralization might be a useful ingredient of diplomacy and will serve as well to disclose those factors in the negotiating situation that determine whether and under what circumstances neutralization can be expected to work. Moreover, since

[1] Parties may have different, even contradictory, reasons for negotiating or establishing neutralization. For instance, one side may envision neutralization as opening the path to the expansion of its influence in the neutralized territory, whereas another side may regard neutralization as a device for removing the neutralized society from the cross-currents of global rivalry.

[2] It is possible that negotiations or proposed negotiations, rather than agreement, are the main objective, as when states seek to convince world and domestic public opinion of their commitment to the nonmilitary solution of international disputes.

94

negotiating neutralization is one instance of seeking agreement in a context of adversity, our understanding of the process can benefit further from the attention paid to it in the work of such conflict theorists as Schelling and Boulding, as well as from the application of conflict theory to the general study of international negotiations by Fred Charles Iklé in *How Nations Negotiate*.

Analytic Considerations

By describing some characteristics of the negotiating situation it becomes possible to make distinctions between different neutralization schemes, distinctions which have consequences for the formation of policy whenever it is a question of determining whether a particular political entity is a suitable candidate for neutralization.

IDENTITY OF THE UNIT

Candidates for neutralization have included cities and waterways, as well as sovereign states. The negotiation of neutralization arrangements for cities is often prompted by considerations comparable to those that lead to proposals for the neutralization of states—namely, conflict avoidance or settlement. Thus, where two or more states claim control over a particular city, neutralization offers a compromise.[3] In contrast, the neu-

---

[3] Neutralization often appears desirable when each of two principal antagonists is concerned less with establishing control over a strategic area itself than with denying control to its rival. In the absence of neutralization it may be that the only way each side could bring about this result would be to establish control for itself. But then a costly struggle would ensue. Neutralization has the advantage that it might avert conflict and at the same time satisfy the real interests of both contenders.

tralization of a great international waterway, such as the Suez Canal or the Straits of Magellan or the Danube River, has as a major additional purpose the sharing of access to a navigational resource that is of value to the community of states. Neutralization is then an alternative to sovereign appropriation and represents an effort by principal states to secure a common advantage.[4] In such a setting, neutralization has many of the same effects and appeals as does the doctrine of the freedom of the high seas.

The main emphasis of our inquiry into neutralization, however, is upon its applicability to states and, hence, upon the effort to protect states by this means from certain destructive forms of international conflict. The states that have heretofore been candidates for neutralization have possessed a distinctly secondary capability.[5] Their strategic importance lies rather in the role they have played in the past as arenas for expansion and struggle for states or alliances that dominate international society or a sector of it. These are the historical instances of neutralization—Switzerland, Belgium, Luxembourg, Austria, and Laos—that we consider most relevant to any present inquiry into the negotiating process.

Usually, the state for which neutralization is negotiated is one whose external security is jeopardized by the

---

[4] For a survey see G. E. Sherman, "The Permanent Neutrality Treaties," *Yale Law Journal,* XXIV (1915), 217–241; cf. also Malbone W. Graham, Jr., "Neutralization as a Movement in International Law," *American Journal of International Law,* XXI (1927), 79–94.

[5] The classification of candidates for neutralization simply as secondary entities glosses over important differentiations among them. The shape of neutralization is influenced by whether the neutralized state has the will, the capabilities, and the geopolitical position to contribute significantly to the maintenance of its neutralization and, also, by the extent to which neutralization entails demilitarization.

competitive aspirations of one or more other states. Where civil strife adds to the dangers arising from competitive intervention—the situation that existed in Laos and prevails now in South Vietnam and Yemen—there is a further problem that may result from the refusal of one or more of the potential guarantor states to recognize the incumbent regime as the legitimate representative of the interests of the country in question. One of the issues central to Vietnamese negotiations, for instance, concerns the form and substance of representation for the National Liberation Front and its relation to the form and substance of representation for the Saigon regime. Thus, the structure of negotiations is likely to be very different if the candidate for neutralization is itself divided into contending factions, each of which has support from some, and is opposed by others, of the various guarantor states.

THE GOAL OF NEUTRALIZATION NEGOTIATIONS

Neutralization may be sought to achieve any number of the characteristic goals of negotiation, as set forth by Iklé.[6] In particular, neutralization may amount to a "normalization agreement"—a termination of an abnormal or violent condition within the society proposed as a candidate for neutralization—as it did for Laos in 1962. Additionally, neutralization almost always has the character of being an "innovation agreement," one that creates a new regime (or status). Occasionally, also, neutralization may turn out to be a "redistribution agreement," in which case the neutralized state acquires certain advantages with respect to autonomy or security in exchange for accepting certain disabilities. The neu-

6 Iklé, *How Nations Negotiate* (New York 1964), p. 41.

tralization of Austria in 1955 was of this latter sort: in exchange for losing the privilege to join alliance systems, Austria achieved the removal of foreign troops from her soil. Similarly, Luxembourg was demilitarized in 1867 in exchange for a great power guarantee of its independence. Finally, negotiating parties may seek "side-effects" by proposing neutralization to convince domestic or world public opinion that a nonmilitary solution is being sought for a situation of actual or potential conflict and that the intractability of the other side is primarily responsible for the danger to world peace and security. Soviet proposals for the neutralization of Germany or United States proposals for the neutralization of Vietnam, for instance, may be susceptible to such an interpretation. When the only goal is to achieve "side-effects," no agreement on neutralization is actually sought or expected; the proposal of neutralization is made an end-in-itself, either to discredit a rival in world politics or to allow the rejection of a proposal to incite greater militancy. Of course, proposals for neutralization may be more or less seriously meant, and it is itself a delicate task of interpretation and perception to assess whether, and to what extent, the aim of a particular proposal is to reach agreement or to engender side-effects.[7]

Neutralization negotiations normally occur in a negotiating context where multiple or overlapping goals are likely to be present. Thus, a state may propose neutralization primarily because it is eager to reach an agreement that brings both normalization and innovation but secondarily because, even if these objectives cannot be attained, it stands to benefit at least from favorable side-

[7] In this respect neutralization negotiations may be usefully compared with arms control and disarmament negotiations.

effects. In fact, the estimate of whether the net product of side-effects will be advantageous to the main parties involved may be a significant factor in determining whether neutralization is potentially negotiable. For instance, in relation to South Vietnam, neutralization may first become negotiable when each of the major parties to the underlying conflict, as a consequence of inconsistent or asymmetrical calculations, anticipates favorable side-effects from proposed or unsuccessful negotiations, rather than when these parties deem the prospects bright for agreement on a neutralization arrangement.

The parties to negotiations may, in addition, have more or less shared objectives. When neutralization is used as part of a general international settlement—as it was at the Congress of Vienna—there may be a common search for normalization and innovation to implement the general policy of stabilizing international society. On the other hand, when neutralization is proposed in a situation of civil strife and foreign intervention, then while one side is seeking normalization the other side may be seeking redistribution. The neutralization of Laos, for instance, may have been viewed by the United States and the Soviet Union as a way of achieving normalization or of saving face, whereas by North Vietnam and China it may have been sought as a means of effecting redistribution or of gaining certain side-effects (such as the removal of the United States military presence). The point is that the negotiating process in situations of the Laotian type will almost surely disclose the different priorities of the negotiating parties, whereas in settings similar to the Congress of Vienna neutralization tends more nearly to express common priorities.

As already indicated, different parties to neutralization negotiations are likely to have different interests and different hierarchies of interests in relation to neutralization. One side may see neutralization as the alternative to "defeat" or to the continuation of a costly and unpopular conflict, the other side as the way to the most rapid and least burdensome "victory." In such circumstances the two (or more) negotiating sides may still properly come to terms on an agreement, for neutralization may serve the temporary, if distinct, interests of all sides. Neutralization in Southeast Asia may be regarded in this light as a rational outcome, depending on the phasing of potentially convergent interests of the adversary parties.

In a situation where perceived interests in neutralization are contradictory rather than merely distinct, it is probable that this gap will become evident in the negotiations themselves. The party concerned with normalization will be more insistent on arrangements supplemental to the status of neutralization that will ensure its maintenance, whereas the party aiming at redistribution may be expected to want to minimize the maintenance machinery and insist that neutralization consist of nothing much more elaborate than the creation of the status.

There are two categories of negotiating parties that can be usefully distinguished: the potential guarantor states and the neutralized state. The concerns of the neutralized state may or may not mesh with the interests of any or all of the guarantor states. In the Austrian negotiations the Austrian government conceived of its interests in such a way that they closely resembled the interests of the Western negotiators while contradicting the interests of the Soviet negotiators. In the Swiss negotiations, on the other hand, there seemed to be a close correlation between the interests of the candidate for neutralization and the interests of all of the potential guarantors. When a widely shared identity of interests exists and it not only extends to the government of the state neutralized but commands the respect of the rest of the society as well, one can be more assured of the longer-term survival of neutralization. But where neutralization is reluctantly agreed upon to gain some other end (the Austrian interest in the removal of Soviet troops, for example) or is used to moderate a conflict and bring order to a society (as in Laos), then the prospects for adherence are diminished.

An additional factor, to be discussed again later, is the balance of capabilities and motivations between the guarantor states and the neutralized entity with regard to the maintenance of neutralization. A city candidate, like Cracow or Berlin, has almost no autonomous capability for preserving neutralization, and the reality of the status is fully dependent on the vigilance of the guarantor powers. In contrast, a neutralized state with defensible frontiers and a strong domestic attachment to neutralization, such as Switzerland, is almost oblivious to the support or role of the guarantor powers. This sort of interaction between the neutralized states and the guarantor states will almost always influence the kind of machinery that is sought or deemed essential to maintain neutralization. The more viable the neutralized state and the more clearly its government conceives neutralization to be in its interests, the less likely it is that anything more ambitious than declaratory status will grow out of the international negotiations.

It seems useful to distinguish between neutralization as a unit event, as a sub-systemic event, and as a systemic event. The three neutralizations of the nineteenth century—of Switzerland, Belgium, and Luxembourg—can be conceived as being of genuinely systemic proportions, for they represented efforts by the principal states to bring added stability to the international system as a whole by surrounding France with a series of buffer states.[8] The neutralization of Austria in 1955 can be thought of as a sub-systemic endeavor to stabilize the relations between the West and the Soviet Union in the sub-system of Europe. Finally, the neutralization of Laos in 1962 can be viewed as an attempt to bring that particular civil strife under a measure of control by insulating the country to a somewhat greater extent from foreign intervention.

One can envision a great power conference in South Africa at some future date where governments will recommend the neutralization of one or more territories in order to bring stability to that tormented regional subsystem, too.

SCOPE OF THE NEGOTIATING SETTING

Negotiations may be conducted with varying degrees of substantive latitude. It may be useful to contrast in this light a negotiating setting in which all bargaining deals are substantively related to the neutralization arrangement itself with those negotiations into which additional subject matter may be introduced.

[8] Where the guarantor states are partly concerned to avoid the use of a neutralized state as a staging area for hostile military operations, total or partial demilitarization may become part of the neutralization negotiations (as was the case with Belgium and Luxembourg).

At the Congress of Vienna, for instance, Austrian acceptance of the neutralization of Cracow was won in exchange for the cession of Silesia and Tarnopol by Russia, while the price for Russian concessions to Prussia with respect to Polish territories was the abandonment of Prussian claims to Saxony. One can, moreover, imagine that neutralization might be more effective in Southeast Asia if accompanied by some kind of wider accommodation with China. In the Middle East, similarly, the neutralization of a Palestinian state (consisting of Sinai, the Gaza Strip, and the West Bank) might become seriously negotiable if accompanied by agreement between Israel and the Arab countries on disputed questions of maritime passage, refugees, river development, and peaceable relations.

In contrast, where a basis for wider agreement does not exist, a restricted scope that corresponds with the area of genuinely converging interests may lead to successful negotiations. The Laos negotiations may have ended in agreement precisely because the issues open to negotiation were restricted. At the same time, the narrowness of the scope of bargaining may have prevented a more stable neutralization scheme from emerging. For instance, one might surmise that more effective machinery for maintaining neutralization in Laos might have been achieved in exchange for a United States commitment in 1962 to refrain from establishing an overt military presence in South Vietnam.

INTERACTION BETWEEN THE WORLD AND
THE NEGOTIATIONS

The subject matter of neutralization negotiations may to a greater or lesser extent be fixed. Negotiating demands and priorities may shift as a result of events that change the perceived ratio of strength and weakness among the parties. The Russians' willingness to agree to the neutralization of Cracow, for instance, reflected their awareness that Talleyrand's diplomacy at the Congress of Vienna had greatly enhanced France's influence at the conference and, generally, within international society.

Negotiation of a neutralization arrangement in the course of an internal war is likewise apt to bear the marks of its dynamic context. Efforts on the battlefield may be directed at altering the balance of capabilities in the eyes of the negotiators and thereby shaping the character of the final bargain. The United States insistence on a cease-fire as a precondition to the Laotian negotiations was evidently prompted, in part, by a desire to foreclose the possibility that military reversals might occur during the negotiations and affect their outcome. Similarly, the French defeat at Dien Bien Phu in 1954 on the eve of the Geneva Conference obviously influenced the negotiations by modifying what various parties to it conceived of as reasonable in the circumstances.

The impact of events external to negotiations may, of course, be much more indirect. One country may be about to have domestic elections, and its leaders may want an international agreement to present to the voters as a token of their accomplishments. Such indirect incentives may shift negotiating demands in either direction, making agreement either more or less attainable.

The longer the negotiations persist, the more likely it is that the general course of international politics and the particular courses of domestic politics in the principal negotiating countries will influence the shape of the negotiations, as well as the attitude of the negotiators toward the goal of neutralization itself. Furthermore, the more unstable the political atmosphere in the candidate country is, the more probable it is that changes within the country will decide the pattern, or even the attainability, of neutralization in the course of the negotiations.

Sociohistorical Considerations

The negotiation of neutralization arrangements appears to reflect basic thinking about the management of international conflict in particular epochs. In fact, it can be suggested that neutralization of secondary sovereign entities is only seriously considered at those times in history during which principal states seek to moderate their rivalries *inter se* through self-conscious diplomacy.

It is striking, and surely worthy of note, that all of the principal instances of neutralization have arisen either in the period following the Napoleonic Wars, initiated by the Congress of Vienna, or in the period since World War II. These periods shared a number of similar circumstances. First of all, a postwar sense of the need to reestablish and maintain international stability through the *conscious* and *cooperative* action of the principal states was prevalent. Second, a strong ideological undercurrent animated international conflict (republicanism versus dynastic legitimacy; communism versus liberalism) and appeared to pose grave dangers of the resumption of large-scale international violence. Third, the ideological dimension of international conflict tended to erode the separation between domestic and international politics, thereby generating serious forms of interventionist diplomacy. Fourth, domestic struggles for dominance weakened the stability of secondary states within international society and confronted these states with the prospect of a loss of independence through intervention.

Having suggested a certain similarity between the atmosphere in Europe after the Napoleonic Wars and in the world after World War II, we must now go on to examine in more detail the factors that prompted neutralization negotiations and the considerations that shaped their specific concerns. This discussion attempts to deal with those features of the international environment that bear on the process of negotiations and should be read in conjunction with the chapter on the history of neutralization.

NEUTRALIZATION AFTER THE NAPOLEONIC WARS

In addition to the celebrated instances of Switzerland, Belgium, and Luxembourg, there were in this period of conference diplomacy a variety of other attempts to use neutralization as a technique of conflict management. To understand how neutralization was negotiated in this international setting, it is essential to grasp the extent to which statecraft rested upon the postulates of the balance of power as these postulates were interpreted by the leading diplomats of Russia, Austria, Prussia, France, and England. The key to international peace was supposed to be "balance," in the sense that no one principal state or coalition among principal states was to be permitted to expand at the expense of the others. In particular, in the aftermath of the Napoleonic Wars there was a consensus on the need to discourage French expansionism. Deterrence took a variety of forms, among which was support for the idea of erecting buffer states to separate France from her chief potential rivals. Part of the purpose of establishing buffer states was to withdraw geopolitically strategic secondary entities from the main currents of international competition, so that no major rival would feel either threatened or tempted by their existence.[9] Neutralization was an arrangement devised to satisfy these functional requirements of the balance of power system.

Thus construed, neutralization was a scheme that was seen to correspond both to the interests of the guarantor states in maintaining the balance of power and to the desires of certain candidates for neutralization to guarantee their national independence against the encroachments of more powerful neighboring states aiming either at expanding their own territory or at thwarting or preempting the territorial ambitions of their rivals. A neutralized state might, therefore, profitably exchange its diplomatic maneuverability for some increased assurance that its territory or its independence would not become an arena of great power rivalry. In other words, if a state was to seek or accede to the status of neutralization, then the heightened prospect of internal sovereignty normally had to be perceived to outweigh the encumbrances on external sovereignty that this status entailed.

[9] "A glance at the map will show that these neutralized states of Belgium, Luxembourg, and Switzerland form a barrier, as it were, between France and the states of central Europe. France had been feared, and such buffer states were thought to be serviceable in keeping her within the established territorial limits. . . . The belief that peace in Europe would be secured by maintaining a balance of power was particularly emphasized in the eighteenth century; and it was maintained that the occupation of any of these buffer states would imperil the peace of Europe by giving to that power advantageous positions which the other powers were reluctant to see in the hands of a possible rival." George G. Wilson, "Neutralization in Theory and Practice," *Yale Review,* N.S., IV (1915), 480–481.

It was just this perception of anticipated reciprocal advantages shared by the guarantor states and the candidate for neutralization that made neutralization a focus for international negotiations in the nineteenth century. The particular shape of the negotiations reflected the relative bargaining positions of the rival guarantor states, the capability of the neutralized state to provide for its own security, and the main problems of maintenance requiring precautionary action to guard against erosion of the status.

The Idea of Neutrality. The use of neutralization as an adjunct to the balance of power was clearly connected with a long preexisting endeavor to limit the scope of warfare through the notion of neutrality, which was designed to implement a diplomacy of impartiality. The development of a neutral status for states that were nonparticipants in an ongoing war represented an evolving effort of international law to reconcile the interests of the general community of states in peace with the claims of the belligerents in victory. The idea of neutrality applied only to a condition of war, whereas the idea of neutralization involved an extension of the policies underlying neutrality to conditions of both war and peace. The rationale for this extension was that the fact of alignment or realignment was itself quite often considered to be a hostile act that could only endanger international peace in a setting where the idea of "balance" was associated with the maintenance of international stability. The neutralization of Switzerland illustrated the establishment of a permanent condition of impartiality for reasons analogous to the logic of neutrality as a temporary condition of impartiality for the duration of a war.

The Status of War. In the nineteenth century, unlike

108

the twentieth, recourse to war was a permissible or, at least, an extra-legal method of implementing foreign policy. Neutralization implied, among other things, a loss of the option to wage war or to participate in collective security operations. A neutralized state was removed from the balance of power pattern of struggle. In effect, the renunciation of force and alignment was exchanged for the guarantee of respect for neutralization. This bargain appealed, of course, only to secondary states—those that could expect to be the victims of expansion rather than the expanders. Belgium and Luxembourg were two such states.[10]

The Response Problem. Neutralization negotiations in the nineteenth century emphasized the status acquired and the attendant consequences. No attempt was made either to establish maintenance machinery or to decide what a guarantor was supposed to do in the event of a violation of the neutralization status. Discussions indicate that the guarantor states did not—except where their own immediate interests were involved—regard protection of the neutralized state from threat, persuasion, or attack as part of a guarantor's obligations.

To grasp fully the nature of the guarantee and the effects of a breach of neutralization, it is important to appreciate the extreme decentralization of international society in the 1800s. There were at that time no international institutions seeking to uphold world peace and security, and the idea of international machinery to implement an international commitment had not yet been seriously envisioned. The expectation was that, if the

[10] For a detailed analysis along these lines, see William E. Linglebach, "Belgian Neutrality: Its Origin and Interpretation," *American Historical Review,* XXIX (1933), 48–72. See Chap. II for information about these historical instances of neutralization.

converging interests that accounted for the original establishment of neutralization were to disappear, the result would be a destabilizing confrontation between rival coalitions of European states.

Lord Stanley, Foreign Secretary of Great Britain, expressed the structure of obligation, with reference to the treaty for Luxembourg, in these terms: "It means this, that in the event of a violation of neutrality, all the powers who have signed the treaty may be called upon for their collective action. No one of these powers is liable to be called upon to act singly or separately. It is a case, so to speak, of 'limited liability.' We are bound in honor—you cannot place a legal construction upon it— to see, in concert with others, that these arrangements are maintained. But if the other powers join with us, it is certain there will be no violation of neutrality. If they, situated exactly as we are, declined to join, we are not bound single-handed to make up the deficiencies of the rest." Such a guarantee obviously has more the character of a moral sanction to the arrangements which it defends than that of a contingent liability to make war. It would, no doubt, yield a right to make war, but it would not necessarily "impose the obligation."

Lord Gladstone in 1870 expressed the policy expectations perhaps even more clearly in his explanation to Parliament of the reasons for the neutralization of Belgium: "In the event of the violation of the neutrality of Belgium by Prussia, France held herself released, and in the event of the violation of neutrality by France, Prussia held herself released. I think we have no right to complain of either power. I think they said everything they could have been expected to say; but we thought that by contracting a joint engagement we might remove the difficulty and prevent Belgium from being sacrificed, and render it extremely unlikely that anything would arise to compromise our neutrality." [11] In effect, Gladstone was presenting neutralization here as a declaratory measure of international order that is dependent for its maintenance upon its general compatibility with the basic interests of the parties joining in its creation. Neutralization, so understood, represents the establishment by formal agreement of a benchmark of normalcy, any departure from which is likely to provoke destabilizing patterns of response from other guarantor powers, although not necessarily in the form of an implementation of the guarantee as such. This analysis applies especially to the examples of Belgium and Luxembourg, since these states lacked the capability to uphold their own status of neutralization in the face of any serious attempt by a principal power to encroach upon it. In contrast, Switzerland gave up no rights of self-protection in the process of becoming neutralized. The abiding Swiss commitment to neutralization, augmented by the rugged topography of the country and by a formidable military capacity to defend itself, has successfully induced all states to respect the guarantee even during periods of utmost turmoil in Europe.

In the nineteenth-century diplomatic setting negotiating states were primarily intent upon preventing violations of neutralization that were easy to discern. There was no general worry expressed about covert extensions of influence through techniques of subversion and infiltration, although there was some sense of danger respecting the defense of dynastic legitimacy and the fear of revived republicanism. As a result, the diplomacy that fostered neutralization arrangements was concerned

[11] Both quotations taken from Wilson, *op. cit.*, 479–480.

with establishing a status in the common interest rather than with providing for its future protection against a determined would-be violator. The massive violation of a status of neutralization in these circumstances would signal the failure of the former attempt to secure the balance and thus would serve as a warning of the need for renegotiations, for war preparations, or for offsetting diplomacy.

NEUTRALIZATION AFTER WORLD WAR II

The two sets of negotiations culminating in neutralization since World War II, the cases of Austria and Laos, have both reflected the tensions generated by the cold war and by the confrontation between the Soviet and Western alliance systems in geopolitically critical sectors of the international system. Neutralization has not been part of a balancing system but instead has amounted to a compromise or stalemate at points of active encounter. Proposals to neutralize South Vietnam or Cambodia reflect similar assessments of the desirability of transforming a costly and dangerous cold war stalemate into something that is, temporarily at least, both less damaging to the state concerned and more promising to the guarantor states. Likewise, suggestions for neutralizing areas mostly outside the cold war setting, such as Cyprus or Kashmir, are largely premised on the mutual desirability of transforming a belligerent stalemate into a peaceful and permanent stalemate. In the contemporary world, then, neutralization functions primarily as a technique of peaceful settlement.

Neutralization may also be relevant to a domestic condition in which there exists a converging interest in terminating competitive interventions prompted by civil strife. The chief intended consequence of neutralization, in these circumstances, may be to remove foreign military participation from the struggle to gain control of the neutralized society, leaving internal factions with the option to fight it out. So understood, neutralization is part of a strategy of deescalation, the aim of which is to decouple national patterns of interfactional struggle from regional or global patterns of rivalry. In such a situation peace may not be the intended result, although to give effect to the negotiations a cease-fire may be arranged. One wonders whether the 1954 Geneva Accords might not have produced a more stable settlement of the First Indochina War if they had provided for a status of neutralization, even given a fair prospect of internal struggle among opposing factions in each of the Associated States of Indochina for political supremacy.

There may, furthermore, be an exchange of detriments that makes the establishment of neutralization more like "a bargain" in which the various interested states each give up something in return for something else. Austria is a good example. The negotiation of a neutralization arrangement after years of agonizing frustration brought about the removal of the Soviet Army from Austrian territory in exchange for an Austrian commitment to remain outside the Western defense system. This bargain was encouraged in 1955 by Austria, then having a government more eager to reestablish the prerogatives of internal sovereignty than to express her pro-Western orientation through a foreign policy based on alignment and collective security.[12] Austrian neutralization subsequently withstood the grant of mass sanctuary to exiles from the Hungarian Revolution of 1956.

[12] See William B. Bader, *Austria Between East and West 1945–1955* (Stanford 1966), 184–209.

This activity by the Austrian government presumably displeased the Soviet Union and could have been relied upon to support a contention that Austria had jeopardized her neutralized status.

In Laos in 1962 neutralization represented the full multilaterality of negotiations that has prevailed in the period since the Sino-Soviet split.[13] Each of the three main negotiating parties perceived neutralization as desirable for quite distinct reasons. The United States sought primarily to stabilize, to the extent possible, a deteriorating military and political situation without having either to accept a Communist victory in Laos or to undertake a large-scale military intervention to prevent it. The main objective of the Soviet Union evidently was both to check China's westward expansion and to remove Laos from the growing area of the United States military presence in Asia. China, one can infer from deed and word, was confident that internal developments subsequent to neutralization would work out to its advantage, bringing into power a friendly, if not a completely reliable, regime. In any event, China (and North Vietnam) retained ease of access to Laos by means easy to disguise sufficient to enable them either to bring decisive influence to bear on the course of domestic Laotian politics or, at worst, to be in a position to offset any unfavorable developments arising from changes in the domestic or foreign situation. The leaders of North Vietnam, too, may have looked upon the neutralization of Laos as helpfully related to their capacity to influence the struggle for South Vietnam.

It seems clear, then, that neutralization in this context

[13] For a detailed appreciation, see the paper by Stephen Fuzesi, Jr., cited in the Preface, on file at the Center of International Studies, Princeton University.

of East-West diplomacy is more closely associated with conflict management than it was in the nineteenth century, when it was mainly an aspect of preventive diplomacy aimed at conflict avoidance. With neutralization oriented now more toward conflict management, there is likely to be an increased stress on implementation and maintenance.[14] The response problem is apt to prove a very important part of the calculations of at least some of the negotiating parties, and the overall plan of neutralization will probably take the form of an international regime rather than of a declaratory measure. In this sense, we are assuming that the Austrian case of neutralization —which, of the modern examples, most closely resembles the nineteenth-century declaratory model—represented the outcome of an unusual opportunity for a mutually advantageous bargain that is not likely to recur.[15] Laos is easily the more prototypical contemporary model of neutralization, for its negotiation was achieved in a context of East-West violence wherein neither side perceived much prospect for a victory at tolerable costs and at tolerable risks; moreover, the society in question, Laos, was not readily susceptible to formal partition.

[14] For example, see criticisms of neutralization for Laos on these grounds in Arthur J. Dommen, *Conflict in Laos—The Politics of Neutralization* (New York 1964).

[15] Germany, too, might seem to provide an opportunity for an Austrian-type bargain, but it would be unlikely to materialize for the following principal reasons: Germany is too significant a state to willingly accept its removal from the patterns of international rivalry; neutralization of Germany would seem to threaten the capacity of the Soviet Union to dominate Europe; and neutralization might allow a reunified Germany to emerge and to renounce the encumbrance of neutralization, thereby endangering Soviet security interests. In short, Germany is too large a potential factor in international politics to deal with through neutralization, a status suited only to states with a secondary influence.

Against this general background there are some factors that stand out as of particular influence in shaping neutralization negotiations at this time in history.

The Status of War. The use of force under present international law is illegal except in self-defense. A neutralized state does not, therefore, give up the option to wage war, as it did in the nineteenth century. But neutralization may restrict the state's ability or duty to participate in the United Nations by eliminating its obligation to help the organization maintain international peace and security. Negotiations to date have not touched on these broad world order issues, although they most certainly will be brought up if neutralization is extended to or proposed for many more states in the world.

Negotiations have, of course, denied neutralized states the option of entering into collective security alignments outside the United Nations. Negotiations have also included discussions about where military assistance is to come from in the event that the neutralized state is not demilitarized. If the neutralized state is allowed to receive military assistance only from either the East or the West, then "neutrality" as an aspect of neutralization is eliminated from the arrangement. Such discretion is possessed by Austria, but not by Laos. There are delicate questions here for which the record of negotiations to date gives no real answers.

Nonviable States. If a nonviable state is neutralized, the protection of the status depends almost exclusively on the joint-and-several commitments and capabilities of the guarantor states. Luxembourg is a nineteenth-century illustration accentuated by the accompanying requirement of demilitarization. The importance of upholding the status will depend on the various incentives that account for the negotiation of a neutralization arrangement. It is easy to imagine that, while one group of guarantor states regards neutralization as a face-saving alternative to defeat, the other side may be viewing it as a prudent step to reduce risks of escalation. Therefore, in this context the negotiations may aim only at *establishing* neutralization and not be concerned with *maintaining* it. For the "defeated" side to seek credible maintenance machinery would be to negotiate a stalemate out of a defeat. In contrast, where the negotiating situation is created and sustained by a sense of stalemate and parity, then bargaining may well shift to the form and reliability of the maintenance machinery. It is true, of course—as Laos might be alleged to illustrate—that, once a defeated side succeeds in negotiating the status of neutralization, it may act to maintain the status subsequent to the agreement and thereby transform the apparent acceptance of a face-saving defeat into a stalemate or something even better.

The Response Problem. With the East-West conflict as the setting conditioning neutralization agreements, great stress is thrown upon the problem of maintenance in the face of allegations and evidences of "indirect aggression" and other forms of covert coercion. The difficulty of identifying a covert violation of a neutralization agreement makes it very hard to disentangle the maintenance machinery from the underlying global patterns of encounter. The result, as the experience of the International Control Commission for Laos suggests, is to introduce the same subjective fact-finding procedures into the machinery as were exhibited in the negotiations. Machinery can thus easily be paralyzed and can only be expected to furnish nominal assurance that neutralization will be preserved. This prospect will be acceptable to the parties if the implicit premise of the

117

negotiations was the use of neutralization as a face-saving alternative to defeat. But if the implicit premise does not exist, or exists to a seriously variable degree for the various sides to the negotiations, then serious dangers of instability will arise from the effort to maintain the neutralization of the state when it is imperiled. There are no easy solutions to this problem, although it would be helpful to clarify the expectations of each party in regard to post-neutralization arrangements. Expectations change through time, and prospective expectations at the time of negotiations may not be transmitted to the future interpreters of a neutralization agreement, especially if there have been significant intervening changes in the policies or personnel of one or more of the negotiating governments. The danger of divergent constructions of what were the essential terms of a neutralization bargain is particularly great in a society driven by political conflict of the kind that includes central disagreement about the proper conduct of foreign relations.

In the present circumstances of hostility and conflict among guarantor states—sharply exceeding the nineteenth-century antecedents—any contemporary reliance on joint action is very unrealistic. If the maintenance machinery is not credible, the guarantor states must expect to rely upon their own capabilities—possibly augmented by coalitions—to preserve neutralization in the face of activity that is perceived to seriously infringe the status.

Since there are few Switzerlands among candidates for neutralization, it is also unrealistic at the negotiations stage to count on the capabilities and will of the neutralized state to maintain its own status. Self-maintenance seems an especially slender reed in the Laos-type situation.

118

A Concluding Comment

The negotiation of a neutralization agreement partakes of the more general circumstance of negotiating an agreement among parties to actual or potential conflict. Many variables give specific shape to neutralization negotiations. Few sweeping generalizations can be reliably phrased. The understanding of a particular set of neutralization negotiations depends on engaging in a configurative analysis of pertinent considerations in the instance at hand. Motivations, perceptions, and expectations of each party to the negotiations, as well as of parties that might benefit or suffer from their outcome, should be carefully limned. Neutralization can be as diverse in impact and form as any other major instrument of statecraft, and the idea of neutralization should never be torn free from its diplomatic setting.

CHAPTER VI

THE MAINTENANCE OF
NEUTRALIZATION

WE SHIFT at this point from the problems of negotiating neutralization agreements to those associated with maintaining them. While the mere negotiation of a neutralization arrangement may produce significant dividends for some of the parties involved, much of the utility of neutralization, from the perspective of managing power in international politics, depends upon the implementation and maintenance of such an arrangement. But the incentives to maintain neutralization are seldom precisely the same as those that led to acceptance of the arrangement in the negotiatory phase. As a result, even the most straightforward neutralization arrangement is apt to be characterized by the development of unforeseen problems affecting the existence, nature, and operation of control arrangements and by disturbing behavior on the part of at least some of the participating parties.

Under the circumstances, it is important to distinguish at the outset between complete and partial maintenance of neutralization arrangements. In fact, very few arrangements dealing with the management of power in world politics actually operate in concrete situations either exactly as they were originally conceived or up to the standards of their ideal type. In the case of neutralization, partial maintenance may take two distinct forms. Some elements of a neutralization arrangement may be implemented successfully while others are not. In addition, the level of effectiveness of the overall arrangement may vary substantially over time. It is important to stress the value of partial successes. So long as a neutralized area does not become a focus of overt and extended confrontation among powers external to the area, the neutralization arrangement retains importance as a device for the management of power.[1] In specific cases, deviations from the terms of the original agreement may alter the proximate balance of political advantages among the parties with interests in the area, but they do not necessarily vitiate the significance of the overall arrangement. Similarly, the fact that the international political system tends to change both rapidly and extensively makes it relatively uninteresting to assess managing devices such as neutralization in terms of the extent to which they tend to perpetuate themselves. Such arrangements are significant primarily in terms of the political setting in which they are formulated. And arrangements that continue in force over long periods generally evolve so extensively in substantive terms that they require reconceptualization from time to time.[2]

The Relevance of Circumstances

The specific problems and prospects of maintaining neutralization tend to vary extensively from case to case.

[1] The case of Laos in the current period is interesting from this perspective. Although the neutralization agreement for Laos is violated regularly by outside powers, the agreement continues to play a role in preventing the country from becoming a focus of overt confrontation among these powers.

[2] Swiss neutralization, for example, has retained its significance from 1815 to the present. Nevertheless, the function of Swiss neutralization is quite different in the contemporary period from what it was in the early nineteenth century.

For this reason, it is difficult to generalize about the maintenance of neutralization. It is, however, possible to distinguish several important circumstantial factors and to assess the impact of these factors on the maintenance of most neutralization arrangements.

The type of area to be neutralized is apt to affect the prospects for maintenance. In this connection, let us return to our earlier distinction among uninhabited areas, inhabited areas without effective governments, and states. Maintenance tends to encounter more and more problems with movement along the spectrum from uninhabited areas to states. Uninhabited areas, such as Antarctica and celestial bodies, offer a number of advantages from the perspective of maintenance including: the absence of local politics creating ambiguities and incentives for outside intervention; few problems concerning intrusions on sovereignty; high visibility of violations; and ease of surveillance. The shift to inhabited areas without effective governments, such as Kashmir or the Gaza Strip, already produces significant problems. Areas of this kind are frequently subject to severe contention among bordering states, and they often possess political factions whose fortunes can be underwritten by external powers. As a result, neutralization of areas of this kind may require guarantee arrangements by nonlocal powers. On the other hand, such areas still have some advantages from the perspective of maintenance since they are generally relatively small and most of the problems associated with sovereignty do not arise. Finally, *states* as objects of neutralization introduce even greater problems for maintenance. These include difficulties associated with sovereignty and political sensitivities affecting such matters as access and information gathering, civil strife aimed at changing the regime of the neutralized state, and various types of outside intervention designed to affect the outcomes of internal upheavals.

Another circumstantial factor affecting the prospects for maintenance is the external political setting. In general, if the configuration of external politics is favorable, extensive upheavals within the neutralized area can occur without jeopardizing the functions of the neutralization arrangement in the international context. Similarly, outside powers generally have the capacity to destroy a neutralization arrangement regardless of conditions within the neutralized area. In assessing the impact of these external conditions, several general factors are relevant. The level of effective community in the prevailing international system is apt to be an important determinant of maintenance. The prospects for maintenance are better in a homogeneous system than in a radically heterogeneous one.[3] Beyond this, the chances of success with neutralization are apt to rise with any shift in the political setting from revolutionary to moderate conditions.[4] Although neutralization may succeed in relatively competitive situations, extremes of revisionism will undermine its viability. Moreover, maintenance is apt to be sensitive to the types of technologies available to outside powers since this factor influences the ease of intervention in neutralized areas.

The impact of the external environment on the prospects of maintenance can be discussed specifically in

[3] For a discussion of the homogeneous-heterogeneous distinction in this connection, see Raymond Aron, *Peace and War* (Garden City 1966), 99–104.

[4] On revolutionary vs. moderate systems, consult Stanley Hoffmann, *Gulliver's Troubles, or the Setting of American Foreign Policy*, published for the Council on Foreign Relations (New York 1968), 17–21.

123

terms of the types of intervention outside powers can practice. Direct intervention, the crossing of recognized boundaries with armed force, tends to be relatively controllable because such actions are highly visible and strongly disfavored by world opinion. Two other forms of intervention, however, are apt to pose major problems. First, indirect intervention is a major problem because of the wide range of forms it can take, problems of visibility and obscurity, and the lack of stabilized norms relating to many forms of indirect intervention. Second, the heterogeneity and ideologically based immoderation of international politics frequently transform unilateral interventions into competitive interventions, thereby introducing obstacles to the maintenance of neutralization arrangements.

A third circumstantial factor affecting the maintenance of neutralization concerns the internal conditions of the neutralized area. Neutralization does *not* aim at controlling or channeling the internal politics or administration of the neutralized area. Nevertheless, internal problems are apt to affect powerfully the maintenance of such an arrangement. A neutralized state that is both well-integrated and stable politically and socially can maintain its neutralized status regardless of the external setting, except in the event of a direct attack in force, such as the German attack on Belgium in 1914, or the onset of a generalized war in the area. On the other hand, a neutralized state undergoing extensive internal upheavals is apt to be ripe for outside intervention and unable to protect itself effectively against such inroads. The result is a spectrum of plausible situations. Whereas Swiss neutralization has seldom been seriously challenged except during the two world wars, the repeated occurrence of outside interventions has constantly threatened Laotian neutralization. And the intermediate cases of Austria and Cambodia [5] indicate the relevance of internal problems in states on the spectrum between absolute stability and full-scale civil war. In the contemporary period, however, the fact that a number of the candidates for neutralization have extensive internal problems must be taken into account as a major difficulty in assessing the prospects for the maintenance of neutralization arrangements. In particular, overt and extended civil strife constitutes a severe challenge to the maintenance of a neutralization arrangement since it facilitates outside intervention and raises incentives to intervene in favor of ethnic minorities, organized movements hostile to the prevailing government, and belligerents in full-scale civil wars.

Finally, many areas that are candidates for neutralization have borderline problems that pose serious obstacles for successful maintenance. Many have border zones that are poorly defined or demarcated, disputed by neighboring areas, remote and hard to reach, porous with regard to the movement of people and goods on an invisible basis, subject to a seasonal or periodic spill-over of ethnic groups, not fully controlled or administered by the prevailing government, or contiguous to a major power. Whereas many of these ambiguities have been clarified in Europe, they are still evident throughout Asia and Africa. And in cases such as Laos, where a number of these problems are present simultaneously, it becomes extremely difficult to guarantee the maintenance of a neutralization arrangement. Under the circumstances, it frequently becomes questionable whether illegitimate outside intervention can even be tracked

[5] Technically, both Austria and Cambodia are only self-neutralized states. Both cases, nevertheless, have considerable relevance to the discussion of neutralization.

down, defined, and assessed—let alone subjected to clear-cut controls. In such cases the need for extensive control machinery is evident. But it is precisely in these cases that it is likely to be extremely difficult to establish and operate control machinery successfully. As the Laotian experience with regard to access, acquisition of information, and interpretation of fragmentary evidence indicates,[6] it is difficult even to ascertain the nature of reality in areas beset with extensive borderline problems.

Roles for Control Machinery

It is important to distinguish between the general problem of maintenance and the specific roles for control machinery in the maintenance of neutralization. Maintenance in general refers to the extent to which a neutralization arrangement is implemented and remains effective. Maintenance may occur in specific cases with or without the use of concrete control machinery, depending upon the configuration of circumstantial factors discussed in the preceding section. On the other hand, control machinery can never provide a substitute for a favorable configuration of international politics within which a neutralization arrangement can function. If the principal parties to the agreement are sufficiently interested in maintaining it, control machinery is likely to be unimportant. Switzerland, for example, has remained neutralized since 1815 without any control machinery at all. If the principal parties do not have significant incentives to maintain the arrangement, however, no amount of machinery is likely to save it. The *de facto* role of the control machinery in Laos, for example, has

[6] For an interesting account that illustrates these problems, see Denis Warner, "A Cautionary Report on Laos," *The Reporter*, XXXIII, no. 10 (December 2, 1965), 35–38.

remained highly circumscribed despite the significant formal capabilities accorded it in the Geneva agreement of 1962.[7]

There is, nevertheless, a middle area between these extremes in which control machinery can play significant roles in the maintenance of neutralization. Such machinery is apt to be particularly relevant when the principal parties have mixed motives that fall between the poles of extreme duplicity and full confidence in the success of the arrangement, when incentive structures shift between the negotiatory phase and the implementation phase of an agreement, and when ambiguities arise during implementation which could undermine confidence if not handled quickly and smoothly. Some examples of roles for control machinery in this middle ground will help to pin down the proposition under discussion here.

To begin with, the very efforts to implement a neutralization arrangement are likely to generate difficulties and ambiguities that will affect the overall viability of the arrangement. Problems of this kind include diverging interpretations of obligations assumed under a neutralization arrangement (for example, the coverage of the concept of indirect intervention), conflicting perceptions and assessments of events, accidental or inadvertent acts, alleged violations denied by the accused party, and testing behavior and borderline acts. In all of these cases, active control machinery may be able to solve, or at least mitigate, problems before they reach the level of rigid political confrontation.

Similarly, there is the problem that might be loosely

[7] For the relevant provisions of the 1962 agreement, see George Modelski, "International Conference on the Settlement of the Laotian Question, 1961–1962" (Canberra 1962).

defined as cheating. If the principal parties have relatively strong incentives to see that a neutralization arrangement does not collapse entirely, obvious cheating is unlikely to occur. But the agreement to neutralize an area is unlikely to exorcise competitive interests entirely. A party may hope to gain the advantages of a neutralization arrangement while continuing to prosecute its own particular interests in the area. Under the circumstances, cheating is likely to be employed when its visibility is low, sanctions are minimal, and disruptive responses from other parties are unlikely. In such cases, control machinery can sometimes minimize cheating that is extensive enough to be politically significant and yet not so overt and unrestricted that it will disrupt the neutralization arrangement regardless of the presence of control machinery.

A third area in which there are roles for control machinery concerns the question of reassurance. Given the various fears, qualms, and mixed motives that the participants in a neutralization arrangement are apt to entertain, it is generally desirable to provide a means of reassuring both the guarantor and guaranteed parties that their respective rights are being adequately maintained. Such reassurance is especially necessary under the conditions of stress or crisis that would arise if, for example, a civil war with ideological overtones broke out within the neutralized area. Similarly, the borderline problems discussed above are apt to produce unsettling ambiguities which would pose a need for reassurance. In general, control machinery with full access to the relevant parts of the neutralized territory can play a major role of reassurance in maintaining the viability of the arrangement.

Other problems stem from the operation of dynamic

128

political forces over time. Even when the initial implementation of a neutralization arrangement is quite
feasible, it must be expected that the balances of political
incentives upon which the arrangement was originally
constructed may shift significantly. Changing conditions
may encourage violations, covert cheating, and acts that
cast doubt on the overall viability of the neutralization
arrangement. Here control machinery may help a neutralization arrangement ride out at least short-term
swings in the balances of incentives and political advantages. In particular, such machinery may aid in
physically isolating a neutralized area from the changing
external political environment and in increasing the
visibility of specific violations until they embarrass the
perpetrator.

In general, there has been little experience with control machinery in the history of neutralization.[8] Formal
machinery was almost entirely absent from nineteenth-
century neutralization arrangements. While the relevant
issues presumably fell within the purview of the Concert of Europe, no formal control machinery was ever
established for Switzerland, Belgium, and Luxembourg.
In the current period, however, there are strong reasons
to consider control machinery in contemplating the potential utility of neutralization as a technique for managing power in world politics. First, the shift from the relatively homogeneous system of nineteenth-century Europe
to the global system of the present period has reduced
the level of effective community underlying interactions

[8] Some aspects of the United Nations experience with peacekeeping operations, however, have considerable relevance to the
problems of neutralization. For a useful survey of United Nations
experience in this area, see David W. Wainhouse *et al., International Peace Observation* (Baltimore 1966).

in the international system. Second, the prominence of ideology has cast doubts on the moderation of international politics in the current era. Third, many of the possible candidates for neutralization at the present time are burdened with extensive problems of internal viability and civil strife which might attract indirect intervention. Fourth, the basic style of international politics in the current period tends to favor the use of control machinery. In an era in which statesmen seldom fail to emphasize the utility of international organizations, at least in general terms, provisions for some type of control machinery are likely to be incorporated into formal neutralization agreements.

Observation and Supervision or Enforcement?

The potential functions for control machinery range from the most circumscribed information gathering to the most extensive making and execution of binding decisions. For the purposes of this study, the most critical distinction is that which separates observation and supervision from enforcement. The key to this distinction is the role of coercion. While observation and supervision can often be facilitated by persuasion, they are activities that do not involve the employment of organized coercion. In the context of neutralization, such activities are associated primarily with periods in which large-scale violations are not occurring. Enforcement, however, refers to the application of organized coercive pressure either to terminate violations or to redress the balance of forces disrupted by major violations. Thus enforcement is a more extensive and demanding function than observation and supervision. In general, it requires a higher level of authority, more extensive agreement among the guarantor powers, greater physical capabilities, and more significant infringement of sovereign rights than either observation or supervision. Therefore, the principal parties to a neutralization arrangement would usually find it easier to set up observation and supervision facilities than to agree on effective mechanisms or procedures for enforcement. This has, in fact, been the tendency in such cases as the International Control Commissions in Indochina, the Neutral Nations Supervisory Commission in Korea, and various peacekeeping operations undertaken by the United Nations where relatively little experience with international enforcement has accumulated in contrast to more extensive observation and supervision efforts.

At the same time, it is important to emphasize the significant links between the functions of observation and supervision and those of enforcement. As the history of Egyptian-Israeli relations in the Sinai after 1956 demonstrates, observation and supervision can reduce the opportunities for significant violations short of overt and organized violence.[9] And there are many situations in which parties that cannot violate an international agreement covertly or under obscure circumstances will refrain from violations altogether. As a result, machinery of this kind is apt to inhibit violations. In addition, observation and verification of violations constitute an important antecedent to effective enforcement. When it is impossible to get reasonably accurate and impartial readings on violations, enforcement may not take place at all or it may be carried out along lines that disrupt the overall neutralization arrangement.

[9] For an account that gives a real sense of the day-to-day operations of observation and supervision in this case, consult E. L. M. Burns, *Between Arab and Israeli* (Toronto 1962).

131

Observation and Supervision

In proximate terms, the activities carried out by observation and supervision machinery are apt to be extremely varied. In slightly more abstract terms, however, it is possible to discern several major themes or threads that generally tie these activities together. First, machinery of this kind is generally designed to provide authoritative characterizations of the nature of reality in the area under observation. This role is far more important than is suggested by the rather simple notion of "fact-finding." Since reality is always filtered through perceptions and since perceptions are shaped by concepts, images, assumptions, predispositions, and so forth, activities of this kind generally become rather delicate even when the observation machinery is not hampered by access problems. Second, observation and supervision attempt to match, on a tentative basis, actualities with relevant prescriptions. Although final matching is often left to statesmen in other arenas, machinery in the field almost inevitably operates to lay the groundwork for matching of this kind. Activities along these lines, however, are also apt to become delicate since normative prescriptions are often ambiguous or obscure in international politics, thereby leaving considerable room for choice in matching actualities with prescriptions. Third, supervision involves the collection of information necessary to check on adherence to accepted arrangements or programs over time. Supervisory activities, therefore, involve the matching of actualities with standards laid down in proximate terms in prior agreements. In a general way, then, observation and supervision machinery tends to focus on the influence that can be derived from

the acquisition and utilization of information and knowl-
edge.

With regard to the maintenance of neutralization arrangements, the most critical problem of observation and
supervision centers on the question of impartiality. It is
important to distinguish between impartiality and neutrality. The machinery under discussion can never
achieve genuine neutrality in the formal sense of exercising no influence at all on the political balances among
the parties to a neutralization agreement. It may, however, achieve a fair degree of impartiality in the sense
of operating without conscious biases in favor of any
party or side. Impartiality is likely to be a function
primarily of the patterns of formal and informal control
that develop with regard to any given set of control procedures and of the prevailing ethos or normative base
which underlies the arrangement. As a result, the crucial
problem in most concrete cases is the effort to achieve
a reasonable degree of impartiality without sacrificing
all effectiveness in performing the tasks outlined in the
preceding paragraph. The trick is to strike a viable balance between the twin dangers of unacceptable bias and
paralysis.

Within this framework, observation and supervision
activities must deal with a number of specific problems.
Given the fundamental nature of neutralization, activities of this kind will generally focus on minimizing
external interventions rather than influencing the internal
politics of the area. A number of specific problem areas in
the establishment of control machinery deserve mention.

Membership. Membership in observation and supervision organizations is important since it directly affects
the possibility of impartiality. There has long been a de-

133

bate on the relative merits of individuals and states as members of organizations of this kind. In the current period, however, the most controversial issue concerns the "troika" principle. Experience with the Neutral Nations Supervisory Commission in Korea and the control commissions in Indochina suggests that the use of this principle in staffing control machinery is apt to lead to operational paralysis. The membership is apt to be a straightforward reflection of the problems that arise in higher-level negotiations. At the same time, however, fears concerning political bias are so strong in the present period that it has generally proven impossible to get agreement on any other principle of membership.

Procedures. Similarly, the procedures used by observation and supervision organizations critically influence impartiality and effectiveness. The most obvious case concerns voting arrangements designed either to reinforce or to circumvent the "troika" principle. Other procedures, including agenda arrangements, techniques of "fact-finding," and the possibilities for appeal to higher authorities, also affect efficacy and impartiality in this area. The core problem is to conduct essentially cooperative activities among limited adversaries.

Access and Physical Capabilities. One of the essential requirements for meaningful observation and supervision under a neutralization arrangement is adequate access to the neutralized area. This is partly a matter of physical capabilities, such as transportation and communications, especially in underdeveloped countries and remote territories. As the Laotian experience indicates, however, it is even more a question of political cooperation. Problems involving access are especially severe when a country is undergoing extended civil strife or when it is effectively partitioned among various factions on a *de facto* basis.

Review Arrangements. There is frequently a substantial need for some authority structure to which observation and supervision organizations in the field can appeal when the local parties to a disagreement refuse to abide by the findings of the field organization or when the problems of control require the exercise of authority at a higher level. Similarly, there are occasions when it would be desirable to allow the parties to a neutralization arrangement to appeal a disputed matter to a higher authority to reduce pressures for recourse to "self-help." The institution of the cochairmanship established under the Geneva agreements of 1954 and formalized with regard to Laos in the Geneva agreement of 1962 was conceived in these terms, but it has proved inadequate because the cochairmen tend to mirror the political divisions of the International Control Commissions. At the same time, it is important to maintain restrictions on the process of appeals to avoid undermining the authority of field organizations through excessive resort to review procedures.

Settlement of Local Disputes. Observation and supervision machinery is not designed to become deeply involved in the actual settlement of contentious issues. Nevertheless, many disputes and allegations arising from a neutralization arrangement might yield to local settlement, especially if dealt with at an early stage. This applies both to disputes between states involved in the neutralization arrangement and to disagreements in borderline situations involving allegations of illegitimate external intervention. Machinery that can move quickly to the actual site of the dispute and is integrated with

135

observation activities might be able to settle many disputes in the local arena before they became subjects of rigid international confrontation. There is an important precedent for such operations in the activities of the mixed armistice commissions (MACs) and in the relations between these commissions and the Truce Supervision Organization (UNTSO) under the general armistice agreements between Israel and the various Arab states.[10]

Just as there are various ways in which the problem areas discussed above can be approached in specific cases, several different structural arrangements can be used in organizing observation and supervision machinery. Each of these structural forms has its own implications for the problems associated with observation and supervision.

National Organization. As has been proposed from time to time, especially in connection with arms control arrangements, it is possible to entrust most everyday activities required for the maintenance of a neutralization arrangement to the neutralized state or states in a given area. Although the resultant operations might require some outside financing, they would have the advantage of being staffed by local personnel familiar with the ethnic, cultural, and political peculiarities of the area. Moreover, such arrangements could be supplemented by outside review procedures designed to deal with allegations concerning failures or biases on the part of the local operations. Nevertheless, this alternative would very likely prove unfeasible in areas racked by

[10] The precise functions of the MACs have generally been intangible and difficult to pin down with exactitude. For an interesting account of their role, consult David Brook, *Preface to Peace* (Washington, D.C. 1964).

severe internal upheavals or ongoing civil strife owing to problems of partiality, access, and veracity.

Autonomous International Units. It is possible to set up *international* observation and supervision machinery composed of individuals rather than states with little in the way of back-up organizations. Arrangements along these lines have certain political attractions since they can be established quite cheaply, negotiated on a relatively superficial basis without reference to various antecedent problems, and set in motion on an autonomous basis to avoid the necessity of constant consultation among the guarantor powers. In simple situations, arrangements of this kind may prove adequate to handle the minimum tasks required for the maintenance of neutralization. On the other hand, such arrangements are apt to be inadequate in many cases since they have virtually no basis of political support in the international arena, little opportunity for appeal to higher authority, and few guidelines for the settlement of internal problems within the organization itself.

Specialized Regimes. Going a step further, it is possible to establish a specialized international regime on a more substantial scale. Unlike an autonomous international unit, such a regime would have states as its members. A regime of this type would therefore be a functionally specialized operation in the manner of, for example, the Danube Commission or the regime established for the Suez Canal under the terms of the Convention of Constantinople of 1888. It would be independent of both existing regional organizations and the United Nations, though it would presumably be compatible with the provisions of Chapter VIII of the United Nations Charter. A specialized regime would reduce the operating difficulties of autonomous units discussed in the previous paragraph. But it could only achieve these advantages at a significant price in terms of the initial advantages associated with an arrangement based solely on autonomous units.

United Nations Arrangements. A fourth alternative is to staff the neutralization machinery with international civil servants or outside individuals of recognized ability and integrity under the auspices of the United Nations. Advantages of such arrangements would include reduced prospects of serious political stalemates, relative depoliticization, and possibilities for improving the processes of recruiting and training staff officers over time. Nevertheless, United Nations involvement would almost certainly prove unacceptable under certain circumstances. If a major party to a neutralization agreement was generally hostile to the United Nations, as China is at the present time, United Nations involvement might never become a serious possibility. Moreover, United Nations operations might prove disadvantageous in other cases owing to the necessity of purchasing political acceptability at the expense of operational effectiveness.

It is evident that there is a wide range of concrete forms of observation and supervision to choose from in specific cases. Moreover, there is little doubt that the ability to match specific arrangements with the requirements of a given situation is likely to be critical in a neutralization arrangement. The twin problems of impartiality and effectiveness, however, underlie all these specific problems and alternatives. In short, decisions on proximate issues can always be assessed in terms of the success in avoiding excessive partiality and extreme paralysis in specific cases of neutralization.

Enforcement

Shifting to the problem of enforcement, we move onto even more difficult terrain. Although formal enforcement provisions have occasionally been incorporated into international agreements,[11] there is little experience with the *application* of enforcement procedures relevant to the objective of maintaining neutralization arrangements in the contemporary international system. Moreover, arrangements requiring drastic measures of enforcement are generally in the process of breaking down or becoming obsolescent in terms of the developing configuration of politics in the relevant arena. For these reasons, it seems appropriate to conclude that drastic enforcement measures do not constitute a major element in the maintenance of neutralization.

Nevertheless, the availability of various restricted enforcement measures may inhibit and control violations arising from the "limited adversary" aspects of relations among the parties to a neutralization arrangement. Even limited enforcement measures, however, require several preconditions if they are to rise above the level of unilateral "self-help" measures. As mentioned previously, arrangements for verification of alleged violations constitute a necessary antecedent to coordinated enforcement. In addition, enforcement requires the presence of political and physical capabilities that can be applied relatively quickly to both the parties and the territory involved in violations. While this does not necessarily imply the presence of standing forces, it does require a

[11] Such provisions, however, seldom go beyond a general pledge by the guarantor states to take whatever actions seem necessary in the event of serious violations of the agreement.

certain amount of preplanning to facilitate mobilization in concrete situations. Finally, coordinated enforcement requires the existence of some form of consultative procedures.

If the guarantors of a neutralization agreement are in fundamental accord, the preconditions of enforcement can generally be met and the problem of enforcement is apt to be minor. In actual cases, however, neutralization is likely to represent only a limited agreement among parties that have major and continuing competitive interests in the neutralized area. Thus, enforcement is apt to be fraught with difficulties. It is frequently impossible to resolve both factual ambiguities relating to alleged violations and disputes concerning the ultimate locus of responsibility for disturbing developments. Because of political biases, normative ambiguities, and the complexities of selective perception, the problem of characterizing actual occurrences frequently leads to rigid confrontations rather than political coordination. These problems become even more disruptive when the alleged violator is one of the guarantor powers rather than an outside state or even the neutralized state itself. In the absence of any higher authority over the guarantor states, therefore, it is frequently impossible to enforce the specific provisions of a neutralization agreement without decisively disrupting the whole arrangement.

These problems raise two additional sets of considerations. First, the possibility of shifting from coordinated to unilateral enforcement actions becomes relevant at this point. Although such a procedure may occasionally be desirable on an *ad hoc* basis, it tends to generate severe difficulties. Unilateral measures raise extreme problems of partiality and often foreshadow, on a *de facto* basis, a reversion to the dangers of the competitive intervention the neutralization agreement was designed to prevent. Such actions, therefore, tend to destroy a neutralization arrangement under the guise of enforcing it. Second, it is important to consider release provisions and arrangements for the resumption of the freedom of action on the part of individual states. Actual developments along these lines may signify breakdown in any specific case. Nevertheless, provisions for such developments may be an important factor in the original acceptance of a neutralization agreement since a party that felt bound to the arrangement even after the occurrence of extensive violations by other parties might find itself severely disadvantaged.

As with observation and supervision machinery, there is a wide range of possible enforcement provisions. Enforcement mechanisms can be planned on a standing basis or formulated as potential arrangements through the use of contingency planning. They can be fully collectivized in the sense of requiring integrated action on the part of all of the guarantor states or decentralized through the utilization of some form of joint-and-several provisions. Or, again, enforcement procedures may be associated with the creation of a special regime on an *ad hoc* basis or tied into the framework for collective action set up by the United Nations Charter. In a proximate sense, moreover, variations along these lines have an important impact on the usability of enforcement procedures in concrete cases. In specific cases, standing forces may involve too much joint planning, while contingency arrangements may be impossible to mobilize with sufficient speed to terminate violations in their early phases. Similarly, collectivized arrangements can be paralyzed by a unilateral or minority veto, whereas

141

joint-and-several procedures are frequently subject to charges of political bias and illegitimate "self-help."

All of these alternatives for concrete enforcement provisions have been debated at great length in various contexts. At a more general level, however, it is important to return to the proposition that, while restricted enforcement activities may well be useful in connection with neutralization, situations requiring drastic enforcement will tend to lead *ipso facto* to the disruption of the arrangement whose enforcement is at stake. Two further conclusions emerge at this point. In most cases, the prospects of preventing or inhibiting violations are apt to be better than the prospects of curbing them once they become extensive and complex. Among other things, this conclusion tends to emphasize the importance of observation and supervision machinery. In addition, there is good reason to suppose that successful enforcement is more fundamentally a function of the basic configuration of politics within a given arena than of the concrete mechanisms established to carry out enforcement measures. For, although variations in concrete mechanisms can be influential in proximate terms, such mechanisms cannot substitute for the existence of a *political* environment in which neutralization is both accepted initially and allowed to continue on the basis of at least partial cooperation over time.

Conclusion

The question of maintenance is of critical importance in assessing the utility of neutralization as a device for managing power in international politics. But it is important to think in terms of various forms of partial maintenance in contrast to the exact specifications of any

142

given neutralization agreement. In general terms, the overall political setting in which a neutralization arrangement is established will determine the likelihood of its being maintained successfully. A number of circumstantial factors contribute to the political setting: the configuration of political relations among the outside powers with an interest in the neutralized area; the internal character and political problems of the neutralized area; and the existence of various borderline problems that attract interventions.

There is a major distinction between the general notion of maintenance of neutralization arrangements and the more specific concept of control machinery. Since formal control machinery was seldom utilized in connection with neutralization in past periods, there is relatively little previous experience to guide efforts now. There are, however, strong reasons to suppose that control machinery may be more important to the success of neutralization arrangements in the current period. The political heterogeneity of a global system, the elements of immoderation in contemporary international politics, and the lack of internal viability of many of the candidates for neutralization indicate a need for effective control machinery. Nevertheless, these same factors tend to throw up serious obstacles to establishing and using control machinery in connection with neutralization arrangements. Thus, for the foreseeable future it seems likely that the relatively restricted tasks associated with observation and supervision procedures will be easier to accomplish than the more extended tasks involved in enforcement.

CHAPTER VII

NEUTRALIZATION: THOUGHTS
IN CONCLUSION

IN THIS final chapter we seek to accomplish three distinct objectives: to summarize the argument for regarding neutralization as a potentially useful instrument of statecraft in the world today; to illustrate this conclusion by indicating how neutralization might contribute to the peace and security of South Vietnam and, more generally, of Southeast Asia; and to set forth some proposals concerning the relationships between neutralized states and international organizations.

Neutralization in the Contemporary World

SOME CONCLUDING OBSERVATIONS ON THE INTERNATIONAL
SETTING AND NEUTRALIZATION

In 1911 an advocate of neutralization, Cyrus French Wicker, wrote that "Neutralization is still a new subject, less than a hundred years old." [1] In 1968 we can no longer claim that neutralization is a new subject, but we can maintain that it is a relatively neglected one in the serious literature on international relations. This neglect is unfortunate because neutralization provides an instrumentality of statecraft that may be able to produce constructive solutions to some of the most troublesome and dangerous conflicts of our time.

The current international setting is constituted in such a way as to make neutralization one plausible de-

[1] Cyrus French Wicker, *Neutralization* (London 1911), 88.

vice for the management of power in international politics. As pointed out in Chapter I, we think of neutralization as one among several instrumentalities available to governments for the management of power. Unilateral or collective military force, alliance arrangements, and quasi-parliamentary diplomacy at the regional and global level are other instrumentalities.[2]

Neutralization as a useful instrumentality of diplomacy presupposes a combination of intense external competition for influence over an area and strong incentives to regulate the competition so as to reduce attendant costs and risks. That is, neutralization represents a negotiated arrangement that seeks to remove the neutralized unit from a zone of intense external competition or, at least, to lessen the prospect of military forms of competition. The consequence of negotiating neutralization, therefore, is to decouple the neutralized unit from international conflict patterns external to it.

A regime of neutralization is not necessarily sought for identical or even similar reasons by different actors. For example, for some actors neutralization may be a way to dislodge an international rival in the neutralized unit preparatory to a strategy designed to establish supremacy for oneself, while for other actors it may be a face-saving device whereby a costly and destructive form of competition may be terminated, almost regardless of whether or not the status of neutralization can withstand subsequent pressures. The literal attainment and maintenance of neutralization, in other words, constitute only one of several objectives that may make

[2] For a more extended discussion of the spectrum of instrumentalities available for the management of power, consult *supra*, Chap. I. See also George Liska, *Alliances and the Third World* (Baltimore 1968), 3–22.

145

serious consideration of neutralization worthwhile. Neutralization, then, is a flexible instrument of diplomacy that, under suitable circumstances, may be used for various objectives by various actors. The essential preconditions for neutralization are that compromise, or the appearance of compromise, be an acceptable diplomatic outcome to all actors concerned and that there exist a sufficiently converging set of perceived interests—although possibly based on quite distinct motivations—to terminate, avoid, or postpone military forms of competition for control of the neutralized unit.

Usually, also, the political elites of the neutralized unit must join in approving a status of neutralization. Depending on the setting, different motivations may account for a willingness on the part of such elites to accept, or even to seek, a neutralized status. There may be more or less congruence between the motivations of the neutralized government and the governments of other states involved. Since a state normally affirms its own sovereignty and since neutralization encumbers the freedom of a government to act, there is reason to suppose that the idea of neutralization will be attractive only to the extent that a state finds its independence and welfare in jeopardy. The most straightforward incentive of the neutralized government is to promote its own autonomy and safety through neutralization. Neutralization may end, diminish, or discourage great power interventions in the affairs of a candidate for neutralized status. However, the status of neutralization may be acceptable only as a short-term expedient to rid the country of one form of outside intervention so as to provide the basis for allegiance to another set of outside actors. For example, one could imagine a Cypriot government agreeing to the neutralization of Cyprus as a way to implement a policy of covert alignment with Greece while inhibiting the prospect of Turkish interference, especially if a network of guaranty were brought into being. Normally, then, representatives of the candidate for neutralization must regard the status as beneficial, although not necessarily in the manifest sense of removing the unit from external competition.

An assessment of plausible motivations of different participants in a neutralization arrangement is essential in considering the applicability of neutralization in any given context. The degree of convergence of interests that support the *actuality*, as well as the *form*, of neutralization greatly influences the stability of neutralization as a device for managing power. Anxiety about manipulative motivations may generate strong demands for enforcement machinery—demands which, other factors being equal, make it more difficult to negotiate neutralization and more expensive and cumbersome to maintain it. The attitudes of the representatives of the candidate for neutralization toward the negotiated bargain will also reflect an assessment of alternative courses of action, an appreciation of the degree of commitment of the guarantor states to neutralization, and a sense of the capacity of their own state to defend its autonomy in a framework of neutralization. Switzerland, with a capability to sustain its autonomy against most forms of external pressure, presents a very different set of national circumstances than does, say, present-day Laos.

The conclusion that we reach is as tentative as it is complex. The acceptability of neutralization depends on the comparative merits of diplomatic alternatives. The stability of neutralization depends on the congruence of the objectives of the guarantor powers *inter se* and vis-à-vis the neutralized state itself. The maintenance of neu-

147

tralization rests on a combination of many factors, in-
cuding the good faith of the guarantors, the capacity of
the neutralized state for autonomy, the will and capability of the guarantor powers to take action if the terms
of neutralization are brought into jeopardy, and the effectiveness of any machinery set up to preserve neutralization.

Neutralization will be the product of a negotiating
process, often undertaken in an atmosphere of extended
conflict. If negotiators are clear about their objectives
and about the costs and risks attendant upon their pursuit of them by means of neutralization, the consideration
of neutralization as one among several diplomatic options appears highly warranted. Neutralization should
never be regarded, however, solely at face value or as
a solution sure to improve upon existing circumstances.
The suitability of neutralization in any given case depends on perceived interests and objective issues. The
neutralization bargain must reflect a congruence between the expectations and capabilities of the neutralized
state and the external guarantors.

NEUTRALIZATION AND PROBLEMS OF PEACE AND
ORDER IN THE CONTEMPORARY WORLD

There are certain features of the present international
system that make neutralization at least an interesting alternative of statecraft and, possibly, an attractive one.
The great powers, especially the United States, the
Soviet Union, and China, are competing in different
ways for influence over small states ruled by governments of restricted capability. These secondary states
are beset by the prospect of internal factionalism and
external intervention. The Vietnam war represents the
culmination of such a combination of vulnerabilities.

Other states in Southeast Asia exhibit similar vulnerabilities.

Once civil war and intervention occur, the military situation may not lend itself to resolution by ordinary means. Such a situation of violent struggle without the prospect of victory for either side may generate a search for a compromise. But the compromise must protect the stalemate reached or anticipated in a military struggle. Under the circumstances, neutralization may offer a device by which to transform a destructive competition for allegiance into a less destructive, or even nondestructive, competitive struggle. The result may be a shift from a battlefield stalemate to a nonviolent stalemate. In the world today there exist several situations of actual or potential military stalemate in which external states have interests antagonistic to one another. Neutralization may also be thought of as a component in a wider political process of settlement, reinforcing, for instance, the acceptance of a coalition government formed out of the domestic political factions previously in violent contention with one another.

The same process of reasoning may apply to competition for control of units in which regional, rather than global, powers are significant participants. The struggle for influence in Yemen, for example, might still be brought under control by combining a proposal for a coalition government with a neutralized status. In this setting regional actors might well act as the principal guarantors.

The most important functions for neutralization today are those of preventing and terminating destructive internal wars that attract significant military intervention from outside states. Unlike earlier eras in which neutralization served usually as a way of effectively removing a unit from a major arena of contention in international politics, the present period is characterized more by competition for political influence and ideological allegiance than by struggle for overt physical control.

Nuclear weapons also enhance the contemporary significance of neutralization. Nuclear weapons underscore the rational limits on the use of violence for political purposes and the dangers of mutual destruction that exist whenever violence is expanded beyond certain limits. There is the possibility, even though it be small, that dominant world states at some stage will actually use such weapons in order to deny the other side "victory." And this very possibility tends to encourage the search for compromise and the effort to transform military stalemates into political accommodations. It is difficult to assess this factor except in specific instances, but it does seem to erode the idea of a national commitment to prevail at any price in a struggle for control in a political arena of secondary importance.

The utility of neutralization as a diplomatic instrument for the management of power is dependent on the specifics of each actual context. There is therefore no substitute for contextual analysis. In these general concluding comments it is only possible to point to certain contemporary realities and international trends that make neutralization relevant and perhaps attractive.

LIMITS ON THE RELEVANCE OF NEUTRALIZATION

There are certain limiting factors that qualify an endorsement of neutralization as an instrument of statecraft in the contemporary world.

Status. The status of neutralized state is not likely to be attractive for many national governments. For one

150

thing, it seems to curb the freedom associated with the full attainment of national independence, especially if neutralization is accompanied by demilitarization. For another, the confirmation of a role for guarantor states suggests some external prerogatives, including possibly even a sort of protective or custodial role. There is, depending on the identity, capability, and expectations of the guarantor states, some danger of neutralization being used as a guise for establishing some form of external domination. Finally, unless other adaptations of the sort suggested in Chapters III and VII are made, neutralization precludes participation in certain collective security arrangements at the regional and global level. On the other hand, neutralization may appeal to states in which government and elites are engrossed in managing internal political, social, and economic development and disdain participation in international squabbles and rivalries.

Scale. Neutralization does not seem to be a viable arrangement for any state perceived by itself or others as playing a major independent role in international politics. A national government with significant capabilities to alter its own external environment is not likely to accept neutralization. For example, Germany presents many of the contextual features that would seem to make neutralization an attractive status, perhaps in order to achieve reunification, except for the fact that it is a powerful state within the European setting.

Minimum Internal Viability. Neutralization is most easily maintained when the government of the neutralized state is able to uphold domestic order under normal circumstances, including some degree of radical domestic opposition. If the government is both ineffectual and beset by a domestic challenger effectively aligned

151

to one or more, but not all, of the guarantor states, then neutralization may prove difficult to sustain. In these circumstances neutralization is not likely to be a political accommodation but a disguised form of victory for one side at the expense of the other. It may be that to disguise defeat is preferable to acknowledging defeat, but the setting is a highly unstable one. In the event that the government of the neutralized state is overthrown shortly after neutralization is agreed upon, there are strong temptations to allege violations of the neutralization scheme and to resume an interventionary competition to prevent a disadvantageous outcome resulting from the internal struggle. These temptations are accentuated if some guarantors regard neutralization as protecting a genuine stalemate and others regard it as a transition device designed to ratify the victory of one adversary over the other.

Implementation. There is some limitation imposed on the efficacy of neutralization when the guarantor states have asymmetrical incentives to sustain neutralization after it has been instituted. Such asymmetries, if perceived, may generate demands for elaborate safeguards and machinery that greatly complicate the negotiating process. If the constituted government of the neutralized state has a firm base of political support and a reasonable competence to govern, external attitudes toward implementation tend to be less important. If international machinery is established to share the burden of sustaining neutralization, then it is essential to assess its adequacy in terms of operating capability and in light of whether its procedures and orientation are compatible with the political consensus reached in the neutralization negotiations.

In general, neutralization arrangements will be unstable if the capability of the government of the neutralized state for maintaining internal order is low and if the guarantor states retain a strong interest in preventing political changes that would be adverse to their whole regional or global position. Still, the overall utility of neutralization can only be assessed in relation to other alternatives. Neutralization may appear highly unstable and yet nonetheless offer the most attractive diplomatic prospect in comparison with other alternatives.

MAJOR PROBLEMS OF NEUTRALIZATION

There are, as earlier chapters have shown, many problems involving the negotiation and maintenance of neutralization arrangements. In this concluding section the most important of these factors will be mentioned briefly.

Change of Internal or External Circumstances. Many changes affecting the neutralized state or the political environment that brought neutralization about may jeopardize a neutralization arrangement. Perhaps the most obvious change of this kind is the rise to power of a regime in the neutralized state that regards neutralization as a betrayal of its basic national interests. Comparable consequences might result from a change of regime or political orientation in one of the principal guarantor states, especially if one element in the change was the charge that the earlier acceptance of neutralization had been a "sell-out" or had been discredited by violations on the part of rival guarantor powers. Changes in both internal and external circumstances, for example, have threatened the neutralization arrangement for Laos in the period since the Geneva agreement of 1962.

Nonassent of a Major Actor. If the neutralization bargain is reached without the participation, or over the objection, of one relevant actor, then its viability may be reduced. For example, the absence of China from negotiations concerning Vietnam might inject this special vulnerability into any pattern of eventual settlement. These difficulties constitute a special case of the general proposition that the depth of converging interests of the guarantors *inter se* and vis-à-vis the neutralized government is an important element in assessing the prospects of neutralization.

Nonfulfillment of Guarantee. Another factor of general significance concerns whether the guarantor states have a reasonably symmetrical view of the nature of their rights and duties under a neutralization arrangement and of the occasion of their exercise. There is on one level the problem of a common framework for collaborative and unilateral action. There is on another level the problem of interpreting ambiguous or disputed facts in the light of this framework. In this situation dangers of *ex parte* interpretation exist if the guarantee arrangements are permissive and decentralized, whereas the dangers of immobility and paralysis exist if procedures are established to achieve impartial or collective interpretation as part of a more mandatory and centralized framework of guaranty.

Neutralization of South Vietnam

The general discussion of neutralization in the first part of this chapter has set the stage for an analysis of neutralization as one element or component in an overall settlement of the Vietnam war. In this context the principal candidate for neutralization is South Vietnam. Under the circumstances, a neutralization arrangement might be useful not only in regulating the dangers of

escalation associated with extended competitive intervention in South Vietnam but also in creating a situation
in which the political conflicts within South Vietnam
could be fought out in a less violent and destructive
fashion.

There is, of course, no point in drawing an overly
optimistic picture of the prospects of achieving a neutralization agreement for South Vietnam. The prerequisites for neutralization in this area have been spelled out
at some length in the discussion of areas suitable for
neutralization in Chapter IV. In general, this discussion
emphasized the difficulties of achieving a convergence of
interests and expectations in support of neutralization
simultaneously among the relevant external parties and
among the various internal factions within South Vietnam,
even though it did not rule out this possibility.

Moreover, even supposing that such a double convergence of interests and expectations were to emerge in a
general sense, the problems of negotiating a specific neutralization agreement would still remain.[3] The problems
of negotiation in this case are serious both because the
conflict in Vietnam has acquired symbolic significance for
other problems in international politics and because constant fluctuations in the assessments and expectations of
the relevant parties would make it extremely difficult
for them to remain united on a particular set of terms
long enough to consummate an agreement. Even if all
the parties are interested in reaching a neutralization
agreement for South Vietnam, therefore, each will also
have diverging and competitive interests which it is
anxious to pursue and which may at times become more

[3] For a more general discussion of the problems associated with
the negotiation of neutralization arrangements, see *supra*, Chap. V.

influential than its interest in reaching an agreement.[4] Under these circumstances, the problem of negotiation hinges critically on the ability of the participants to gauge the phases of the conflict or bargaining process accurately and to time diplomatic initiatives to take advantage of the shifting complexion of the conflict. The same initiative that succeeds when the perspectives and expectations of the relevant parties are momentarily congruent, for example, may fail entirely when this condition does not hold and may thereby generate important impediments to negotiation in subsequent phases.

Several more specific problems associated with the negotiating process are also relevant to the prospects of neutralizing South Vietnam. The fact that the situation involves a protracted war increases the problems of the negotiating process considerably. Under the circumstances, any negotiations concerning neutralization are almost certain to become highly visible; the actions of the parties are bound to acquire far-reaching symbolic content; the competitive interests of the participants are likely to be emphasized by many decisionmakers; and the level of mutual suspicion is apt to be high. In addition, bargaining tactics employed by all the relevant parties are bound to condition the negotiating process in a situation of this kind. The resultant impediments to negotiation include the rigidities associated with a mutual employment of committal tactics and fears of demonstrating weakness through offers of concessions or efforts to take the first step toward serious negotiations. Problems of this kind can sometimes be dealt with constructively by intermediaries. And there may well be

---

[4] The problem here is essentially the same as that posed by Rousseau in his story of the five hunters pursuing a deer.

significant roles for intermediaries in any serious effort to negotiate a neutralization arrangement for South Vietnam.

Thus, the problems of achieving neutralization for South Vietnam are extensive. Assuming, however, that a neutralization arrangement could be worked out for South Vietnam, what would its principal consequences be? For South Vietnam itself the consequences would clearly vary with the effectiveness and longevity of the arrangement. And neither of these are factors that can be fully determined in advance. Moreover, although such an arrangement would reduce the impact of external intervention on the internal politics of South Vietnam, there is nothing in the nature of neutralization that would necessitate a cessation of civil strife within South Vietnam. In fact, successful neutralization would provide a framework within which a process of political shakedown could take place without endangering international peace and security. Nevertheless, even though the resultant process might well involve violence of substantial proportions,[5] the violence would no doubt be less extensive than that associated with competitive intervention. Under the circumstances, the outcome would constitute the closest approximation to self-determination that South Vietnam is likely to achieve in the foreseeable future.

Furthermore, there is nothing in neutralization that would preclude an eventual reunification of North and

[5] The recent cases of Indonesia and Nigeria illustrate the point that large-scale violence may well characterize political upheavals even in the absence of external intervention. These cases are also illustrations, however, of the point that large-scale violence in the absence of competitive intervention does not constitute a serious threat to the stability of the international system.

South Vietnam. Neutralization would, though, place important restrictions on the processes through which reunification could be achieved. To the extent that neutralization was effectively implemented, any move toward reunification would have to arise from political processes inside South Vietnam rather than from direct or indirect pressures projected into the area by outside powers. And while these restrictions would no doubt be difficult to maintain in some situations, they might have major consequences for the future of South Vietnam. For example, it is possible that South Vietnam might opt for independence regardless of the composition of the regime that ultimately came to power in the area.

It is also useful to consider the implications for the management of power in international politics that would flow from an agreement to neutralize South Vietnam. First, neutralization represents a device by which to minimize the impact of the Vietnam war on international bargaining reputations, commitments, and the basic rules of the game in international politics. Neither side would decisively win or lose the Vietnam war.[6] On the contrary, the result would be ambiguous and fuzzy enough to allow for a variety of interpretations, a fact that would tend to reduce the impact of Vietnam on other arenas of international contention. This is why perceived stalemate was classified in Chapter IV as a prerequisite for neutralization in Vietnam. For, while neutralization may appear to all relevant parties as an attractive device for terminating a stalemate, it is hardly likely to appeal to

[6] It is possible that a party originally supported by one of the intervening states would emerge victorious at the end of the civil upheavals. To reach this point, however, would take some time, during which various ambiguities and intervening events might tend to obscure the original picture.

a party determined to engage in a symbolic test of strength which it believes it can win decisively.[7]

Second, several questions concerning regional relationships in Southeast Asia are raised by the prospect of neutralizing South Vietnam. The political characteristics of this region might well make it difficult to implement successfully a neutralization arrangement for South Vietnam alone. The region does not at present have stable regional arrangements for the management of power. It includes several states that may not prove viable internally as well as several long-standing axes of interstate contention. The regional setting, therefore, might generate both incentives and opportunities for new interventions in South Vietnam following formal neutralization. At the same time, however, a successful neutralization of South Vietnam might produce, at least temporarily, important advantages for the management of power within Southeast Asia itself. The traditional problems of managing power in this region have arisen from the expansionist drive of the Vietnamese people whenever they have been more or less united among themselves.[8] Conflict in Southeast Asia has frequently polarized around a Thai-Viet (or East-West) axis. Insofar as the neutralization of South Vietnam were to provide an alternative to a strong, unified, and expansionist Vietnam, therefore,

[7] It is possible, for example, that the Chinese regard the Vietnam war as a decisive test case for their theory of wars of national liberation. And this feeling may well be exacerbated by the striking failures of Chinese foreign policy in other areas in the years since 1965. If this is the case, it is likely that the Chinese will attempt to exert pressure on North Vietnam to carry the war to a decisive conclusion.

[8] For an interesting discussion of these traditional problems of managing power in Southeast Asia, consult John T. McAlister, Jr., "The Possibilities for Diplomacy in Southeast Asia," *World Politics*, XIX, no. 2 (January 1967), 258–305.

such an arrangement might be useful in regulating the traditional sources of disruption in the politics of Southeast Asia. And the regulatory procedures in this case would certainly be less costly and destructive than the traditional source of regulation—extended civil strife among the Vietnamese people.

Third, the neutralization of South Vietnam might open the way to negotiation on several more general issues concerning the management of power in Southeast Asia which the Vietnam war has either generated or exacerbated. Thus, the neutralization of South Vietnam might produce both the incentives and the preconditions for the negotiation of further arrangements on such questions as the strengthening of the neutralization arrangement for Laos, the formalization of Cambodian self-neutralization, and a *de facto* deal on Thailand based on a withdrawal of American troops in exchange for meaningful arrangements designed to minimize external support for indigenous insurgents in the country. In addition, these proximate political arrangements might well open the way for an organized program of economic and political development for Southeast Asia,[9] an outcome that may well be necessary (though not sufficient) for success in efforts to manage power in the area over the long run. In particular, the need to develop impartial mechanisms for the channeling of external assistance to the neutralized states of Southeast Asia might provide the necessary spur for initial efforts to coordinate a program of economic and political development for the area.

[9] The United Nations machinery for Southeast Asia (i.e., ECAFE and the Mekong River project) might be useful as bases for a more systematic program. In addition, the United States has expressed an interest in carrying out such a program in the aftermath of the Vietnam war. This interest was first expressed formally in President Johnson's speech at Johns Hopkins University on April 7, 1965.

Finally, the neutralization of South Vietnam might have important effects on the orientations of major external powers, such as the United States, the Soviet Union, and China, toward the problems of managing power in Southeast Asia. If all three of these powers were to unite on a neutralization arrangement for South Vietnam, the opportunities for both Chinese expansionism and excessive American intervention in the area would be reduced. As a result, the management of power in Southeast Asia would become closely tied to the configuration of power among the local parties and the development of local arrangements for the management of power. In this connection, the prospects of avoiding a sharp polarization of conflict around the Thai-Viet axis would become particularly important. On the other hand, achievement of the neutralization of South Vietnam without the participation of China would signify, in effect, a movement toward coordination on the part of the Soviet Union, North Vietnam, and the United States in the interests of creating a balance to the weight of Chinese influence in Southeast Asia.[10] Under these circumstances, the external powers would remain deeply involved in Southeast Asia, but the pattern of their involvement would be altered. The result might be movement toward a double balance of power for Southeast Asia (involving both the great powers and the local powers),[11] in contrast to the dangerous combination of

[10] For a more extended discussion of this possibility, see Oran R. Young, "Political Discontinuities in the International System," *World Politics,* XX, no. 3 (April 1968), 369–392.

[11] The notion of a *double* balance refers here to the conjunction of a rough balance of power among the major external powers with regard to their interests in Southeast Asia and a local balance of power among the states of Southeast Asia themselves. For an interesting discussion of this theme, see Coral Bell, "The Asian Balance

civil strife within local states and competitive intervention on the part of external powers that exists at the present time.

Neutralized States and International Organizations

If a formal international status of permanent neutrality is to be adopted as a useful means of managing power in certain types of international situations, attention should be given to the relationship of neutralized states to international organizations. This is a serious problem because a neutralized state is obligated to abstain from military intervention in other states and also from any action that might at some future time involve it in hostilities. A state with such obligations cannot participate in international organizations whose members are required to undertake military, political, or economic sanctions against other states or to vote on issues regarded by major competing coalitions of states as critical to their political role.

Switzerland faced this problem in the League of Nations and experimented unsuccessfully with a status of "qualified" neutrality which released it from the obligation to participate in military, as distinct from economic, sanctions. When the United Nations was established, the Swiss government decided not to seek admission because of the apparent incompatibility between the obligations of membership and those of permanent neutrality. This question has not been raised in connection with Austrian and Laotian membership in the United Nations, but neither has it been resolved in such a man-

of Power," Adelphi Paper No. 44 (Institute for Strategic Studies, February 1968).

ner as to provide a stable basis for the formal establishment of an international status of permanent neutrality.

Neutralized states face a number of problems as members of the United Nations. The fundamental problem is confronted in Article 2, paragraph 5 of the Charter, which states that "All Members shall give the United Nations every assistance in any action it takes in accordance with the present Charter, and shall refrain from giving assistance to any state against which the United Nations is taking preventive or enforcement action." The incompatibility of this obligation with a status of permanent neutrality was explicitly noted at the San Francisco Conference at which the Charter was adopted, and the vote on this paragraph was understood to exclude the possibility that a neutralized state could escape from this obligation.[12]

A further problem is represented by the provision in Articles 39–43 that the Security Council may take measures, including the use of armed force, to implement its decisions with respect to threats to the peace, breaches of the peace, and acts of aggression. No state is in principle exempt from being asked to participate in military measures, although the contribution of armed forces to the maintenance of international peace and security is subject to special agreements concluded between the Security Council and member states. Participation in military sanctions is thus not mandatory, but the ability of a member state to avoid such participation depends on the understanding and good will of the Security Council. In the event of an international dispute in an area

[12] This question is discussed in Hans Kelsen, *The Law of the United Nations* (London 1950), 94; and in J. F. Lalive, "International Organization and Neutrality," *British Year Book of International Law*, XXIV (1947), 72–89.

adjacent to a neutralized state, or under circumstances in which the members of the Security Council were not sympathetic to the obligations of permanent neutrality, such a state might find it difficult to reconcile its two sets of obligations. Nonmilitary measures that might be recommended by the Security Council would, of course, not involve acts of belligerency, but they would nevertheless be difficult to reconcile with the obligation of a neutralized state to avoid policies that might at some future time involve it in hostilities.[13]

Apart from these strictly legal questions regarding the compatibility between permanent neutrality and membership in the United Nations, there are also significant political questions. Although the recommendations of the General Assembly are not mandatory, numerous occasions arise in which votes are taken that require member states to side with one or another of the major rival groupings of member states. In some cases even abstentions are interpreted as the expression of a position regarding the political issues that divide member states. Under conditions of international tension, a neutralized state might find it difficult to avoid siding with one or another of the parties to a dispute. Since controversial votes of this type are most likely to occur in the Security Council, it may be questioned whether a neutralized state should be eligible for election to the Security Council or should vote in the General Assembly on

[13] There have been several studies of these issues in connection with the Austrian case: Alfred Verdross, "Austria's Permanent Neutrality and the United Nations Organization," *American Journal of International Law*, L (January 1956), 61–68; Felix Ermacora, *Österreichs Staatsvertrag und Neutralität* (Frankfurt am Main 1957); and especially Wolfgang Strasser, *Österreich und die Vereinten Nationen* (Vienna 1967), 34–49.

the critical issues requiring a two-thirds majority of the members present and voting.

These problems suggest that, for permanent neutrality to be accepted as a formal international status, arrangements should be made to adapt the Charter to this potentially small, but nevertheless important, category of states. A full protection of the status of permanent neutrality in the United Nations would require an understanding to the effect that neutralized states would not be eligible for membership in the Security Council, would not be called upon to participate in military or nonmilitary actions called for under Articles 41–43, and would not be expected to participate in votes in the General Assembly, even in the form of abstentions, in cases where participation might involve taking sides on major political issues.

The Charter offers two possibilities for giving effect to an exceptional treatment of this type for member states enjoying a status of permanent neutrality. Article 48 provides that, for the maintenance of international peace and security, the Security Council may call for participation "by all the Members" or "by some of them," as it may determine. This option suggests that the Security Council has the authority to exempt states from participating in the implementation of its decisions and that neutralized states might be so exempted. An exemption of this type might indeed be made in regard to any particular dispute; but it was not the intention of the Charter to exempt neutralized states, and the Security Council might at any time revert to a policy hostile to the obligations of permanent neutrality.

A more satisfactory solution, although one more difficult to achieve, would be to amend the Charter under the provisions of Article 108 with a view to formalizing an exceptional status within the United Nations of neutralized states along the lines suggested. Such a solution would serve to recognize the importance of the role that permanent neutrality can play as a special means of preserving international order and, at the same time, would permit neutralized states to participate in the international organization to the extent permitted by the obligations of permanent neutrality.

APPENDICES

DECLARATION ON THE
NEUTRALITY OF LAOS

The Governments of the Union of Burma, the Kingdom of Cambodia, Canada, the People's Republic of China, the Democratic Republic of Viet-Nam, the Republic of France, the Republic of India, the Polish People's Republic, the Republic of Viet-Nam, the Kingdom of Thailand, the Union of Soviet Socialist Republics, the United Kingdom of Great Britain and Northern Ireland and the United States of America, whose representatives took part in the International Conference on the Settlement of the Laotian Question, 1961–1962;

Welcoming the presentation of the statement of neutrality by the Royal Government of Laos of July 9, 1962, and taking note of this statement, which is, with the concurrence of the Royal Government of Laos, incorporated in the present Declaration as an integral part thereof, and the text of which is as follows:

THE ROYAL GOVERNMENT OF LAOS,

Being resolved to follow the path of peace and neutrality in conformity with the interests and aspirations of the Laotian people, as well as the principles of the Joint Communiqué of Zurich dated June 22, 1961, and of the Geneva Agreements of 1954, in order to build a peaceful, neutral, independent, democratic, unified and prosperous Laos,

Solemnly declares that:

(1) It will resolutely apply the five principles of peaceful co-existence in foreign relations, and will develop friendly relations and establish diplomatic relations with all countries. the neighbouring countries first

and foremost, on the basis of equality and of respect for the independence and sovereignty of Laos;

(2) It is the will of the Laotian people to protect and ensure respect for the sovereignty, independence, neutrality, unity, and territorial integrity of Laos;

(3) It will not resort to the use or threat of force in any way which might impair the peace of other countries, and will not interfere in the internal affairs of other countries;

(4) It will not enter into any military alliance or into any agreement, whether military or otherwise, which is inconsistent with the neutrality of the Kingdom of Laos; it will not allow the establishment of any foreign military base on Laotian territory, nor allow any country to use Laotian territory for military purposes or for the purposes of interference in the internal affairs of other countries, nor recognise the protection of any alliance or military coalition, including SEATO.

(5) It will not allow any foreign interference in the internal affairs of the Kingdom of Laos in any form whatsoever;

(6) Subject to the provisions of Article 5 of the Protocol, it will require the withdrawal from Laos of all foreign troops and military personnel, and will not allow any foreign troops or military personnel to be introduced into Laos;

(7) It will accept direct and unconditional aid from all countries that wish to help the Kingdom of Laos build up an independent and autonomous national economy on the basis of respect for the sovereignty of Laos;

(8) It will respect the treaties and agreements signed in conformity with the interests of the Laotian

people and of the policy of peace and neutrality of the Kingdom, in particular the Geneva Agreements of 1962, and will abrogate all treaties and agreements which are contrary to those principles.

This statement of neutrality by the Royal Government of Laos shall be promulgated constitutionally and shall have the force of law.

The Kingdom of Laos appeals to all the States participating in the International Conference on the Settlement of the Laotian Question, and to all other States, to recognise the sovereignty, independence, neutrality, unity and territorial integrity of Laos, to conform to these principles in all respects, and to refrain from any action inconsistent therewith.

Confirming the principles of respect for the sovereignty, independence, unity and territorial integrity of the Kingdom of Laos and non-interference in its internal affairs which are embodied in the Geneva Agreements of 1954;

Emphasising the principle of respect for the neutrality of the Kingdom of Laos;

Agreeing that the above-mentioned principles constitute a basis for the peaceful settlement of the Laotian question;

Profoundly convinced that the independence and neutrality of the Kingdom of Laos will assist the peaceful democratic development of the Kingdom of Laos and the achievement of national accord and unity in that country, as well as the strengthening of peace and security in South-East Asia;

1. Solemnly declare, in accordance with the will of the Government and people of the Kingdom of Laos, as expressed in the statement of neutrality by the Royal Government of Laos of July 9, 1962, that they recognise

171

and will respect and observe in every way the sovereignty, independence, neutrality, unity and territorial integrity of the Kingdom of Laos.

2.   Undertake, in particular, that

(*a*) they will not commit or participate in any way in any act which might directly or indirectly impair the sovereignty, independence, neutrality, unity or territorial integrity of the Kingdom of Laos;

(*b*) they will not resort to the use or threat of force or any other measure which might impair the peace of the Kingdom of Laos;

(*c*) they will refrain from all direct or indirect interference in the internal affairs of the Kingdom of Laos;

(*d*) they will not attach conditions of a political nature to any assistance which they may offer or which the Kingdom of Laos may seek;

(*e*) they will not bring the Kingdom of Laos in any way into any military alliance or any other agreement, whether military or otherwise, which is inconsistent with her neutrality, nor invite or encourage her to enter into any such alliance or to conclude any such agreement;

(*f*) they will respect the wish of the Kingdom of Laos not to recognise the protection of any alliance or military coalition, including SEATO;

(*g*) they will not introduce into the Kingdom of Laos foreign troops or military personnel in any form whatsoever, nor will they in any way facilitate or connive at the introduction of any foreign troops or military personnel;

(*h*) they will not establish nor will they in any way facilitate or connive at the establishment in the

Kingdom of Laos of any foreign military base, foreign strong point or other foreign military installation of any kind;

(*i*) they will not use the territory of the Kingdom of Laos for interference in the internal affairs of other countries;

(*j*) they will not use the territory of any country, including their own for interference in the internal affairs of the Kingdom of Laos.

3. Appeal to all other States to recognise, respect and observe in every way the sovereignty, independence and neutrality, and also the unity and territorial integrity, of the Kingdom of Laos and to refrain from any action inconsistent with these principles or with other provisions of the present Declaration.

4. Undertake, in the event of a violation or threat of violation of the sovereignty, independence, neutrality, unity or territorial integrity of the Kingdom of Laos, to consult jointly with the Royal Government of Laos and among themselves in order to consider measures which might prove to be necessary to ensure the observance of these principles and the other provisions of the present Declaration.

5. The present Declaration shall enter into force on signature and together with the statement of neutrality by the Royal Government of Laos of July 9, 1962, shall be regarded as constituting an international agreement. The present Declaration shall be deposited in the archives of the Governments of the United Kingdom and the Union of Soviet Socialist Republics, which shall furnish certified copies thereof to the other signatory States and to all the other States of the world.

In witness whereof, the undersigned Plenipotentiaries have signed the present Declaration.

Done in two copies in Geneva this twenty-third day of July one thousand nine hundred and sixty-two in the English, Chinese, French, Laotian and Russian languages, each text being equally authoritative.

PROTOCOL TO THE DECLARATION
ON THE NEUTRALITY OF LAOS

The Governments of the Union of Burma, the Kingdom of Cambodia, Canada, the People's Republic of China, the Democratic Republic of Viet-Nam, the Republic of France, the Republic of India, the Kingdom of Laos, the Polish People's Republic, the Republic of Viet-Nam, the Kingdom of Thailand, the Union of Soviet Socialist Republics, the United Kingdom of Great Britain and Northern Ireland and the United States of America;

Having regard to the Declaration on the Neutrality of Laos of July 23, 1962;

Have agreed as follows:

ARTICLE 1

For the purposes of this Protocol

(a) the term "foreign military personnel" shall include members of foreign military missions, foreign military advisers, experts, instructors, consultants, technicians, observers and any other foreign military persons, including those serving in any armed forces in Laos, and foreign civilians connected with the supply, maintenance, storing and utilization of war materials;

(b) the term "the Commission" shall mean the International Commission for Supervision and Control in Laos set up by virtue of the Geneva Agreements of 1954 and composed of the representatives of Canada, India and Poland, with the representative of India as Chairman;

(c) the term "the Co-Chairmen" shall mean the Co-Chairmen of the International Conference for the

175

Settlement of the Laotian Question, 1961–1962, and their successors in the offices of Her Britannic Majesty's Principal Secretary of State for Foreign Affairs and Minister for Foreign Affairs of the Union of Soviet Socialist Republics respectively;

(d) the term "the members of the Conference" shall mean the Governments of countries which took part in the International Conference for the Settlement of the Laotian Question, 1961–1962.

ARTICLE 2

All foreign regular and irregular troops, foreign para-military formations and foreign military personnel shall be withdrawn from Laos in the shortest time possible and in any case the withdrawal shall be completed not later than thirty days after the Commission has notified the Royal Government of Laos that in accordance with Articles 3 and 10 of this Protocol its inspection teams are present at all points of withdrawal from Laos. These points shall be determined by the Royal Government of Laos in accordance with Article 3 within thirty days after the entry into force of this Protocol. The inspection teams shall be present at these points and the Commission shall notify the Royal Government of Laos thereof within fifteen days after the points have been determined.

ARTICLE 3

The withdrawal of foreign regular and irregular troops, foreign para-military formations and foreign military personnel shall take place only along such routes and through such points as shall be determined by the Royal Government of Laos in consultation with the Commission. The Commission shall be notified in advance of the point and time of all such withdrawals.

ARTICLE 4

The introduction of foreign regular and irregular troops, foreign para-military formations and foreign military personnel into Laos is prohibited.

ARTICLE 5

Note is taken that the French and Laotian Governments will conclude as soon as possible an arrangement to transfer the French military installations in Laos to the Royal Government of Laos.

If the Laotian Government considers it necessary, the French Government may as an exception leave in Laos for a limited period of time a precisely limited number of French military instructors for the purpose of training the armed forces of Laos.

The French and Laotian Governments shall inform the members of the Conference, through the Co-Chairmen, of their agreement on the question of the transfer of the French military installations in Laos and of the employment of French military instructors by the Laotian Government.

ARTICLE 6

The introduction into Laos of armaments, munitions and war material generally, except such quantities of conventional armaments as the Royal Government of Laos may consider necessary for the national defence of Laos, is prohibited.

ARTICLE 7

All foreign military persons and civilians captured or interned during the course of hostilities in Laos shall be released within thirty days after the entry into force of this Protocol and handed over by the Royal Government of Laos to the representatives of the Governments of the countries of which they are nationals in order that they may proceed to the destination of their choice.

ARTICLE 8

The Co-Chairmen shall periodically receive reports from the Commission. In addition the Commission shall immediately report to the Co-Chairmen any violations or threats of violations of this Protocol, all significant steps which it takes in pursuance of this Protocol, and also any other important information which may assist the Co-Chairmen in carrying out their functions. The Commission may at any time seek help from the Co-Chairmen in the performance of its duties, and the Co-Chairmen may at any time make recommendations to the Commission exercising general guidance.

The Co-Chairmen shall circulate the reports and any other important information from the Commission of the members of the Conference.

The Co-Chairmen shall exercise supervision over the observance of this Protocol and the Declaration on the Neutrality of Laos.

The Co-Chairmen will keep the members of the Conference constantly informed and when appropriate will consult with them.

ARTICLE 9

The Commission shall, with the concurrence of the Royal Government of Laos, supervise and control the cease-fire in Laos.

The Commission shall exercise these functions in full co-operation with the Royal Government of Laos and within the framework of the Cease-Fire Agreement or cease-fire arrangements made by the three political forces in Laos, or the Royal Government of Laos. It is understood that responsibility for the execution of the cease-fire shall rest with the three parties concerned and with the Royal Government of Laos after its formation.

ARTICLE 10

The Commission shall supervise and control the withdrawal of foreign regular and irregular troops, foreign para-military formations and foreign military personnel. Inspection teams sent by the Commission for these purposes shall be present for the period of the withdrawal at all points of withdrawal from Laos determined by the Royal Government of Laos in consultation with the Commission in accordance with Article 3 of this Protocol.

ARTICLE 11

The Commission shall investigate cases where there are reasonable grounds for considering that a violation of the provisions of Article 4 of this Protocol has occurred.

It is understood that in the exercise of this function the Commission is acting with the concurrence of the Royal Government of Laos. It shall carry out its investigations in full co-operation with the Royal Government of Laos and shall immediately inform the Co-Chairmen of any violations or threats of violations of Article 4, and also of all significant steps which it takes in pursuance of this Article in accordance with Article 8.

ARTICLE 12

The Commission shall assist the Royal Government of Laos in cases where the Royal Government of Laos con-

179

siders that a violation of Article 6 of this Protocol may have taken place. This assistance will be rendered at the request of the Royal Government of Laos and in full co-operation with it.

ARTICLE 13

The Commission shall exercise its functions under this Protocol in close co-operation with the Royal Government of Laos. It is understood that the Royal Government of Laos at all levels will render the Commission all possible assistance in the performance by the Commission of these functions and also will take all necessary measures to ensure the security of the Commission and its inspection teams during their activities in Laos.

ARTICLE 14

The Commission functions as a single organ of the International Conference for the Settlement of the Laotian Question, 1961–1962. The members of the Commission will work harmoniously and in co-operation with each other with the aim of solving all questions within the terms of reference of the Commission.

Decisions of the Commission on questions relating to violations of Articles 2, 3, 4 and 6 of this Protocol or of the cease-fire referred to in Article 9, conclusions on major questions sent to the Co-Chairmen and all recommendations by the Commission shall be adopted unanimously. On other questions, including procedural questions, and also questions relating to the initiation and carrying out of investigations (Article 15), decisions of the Commission shall be adopted by majority vote.

ARTICLE 15

In the exercise of its specific functions which are laid down in the relevant articles of this Protocol the Commission shall conduct investigations (directly or by sending inspection teams), when there are reasonable grounds for considering that a violation has occurred. These investigations shall be carried out at the request of the Royal Government of Laos or on the initiative of the Commission, which is acting with the concurrence of the Royal Government of Laos.

In the latter case decisions on initiating and carrying out such investigations shall be taken in the Commission by majority vote.

The Commission shall submit agreed reports on investigations in which differences which may emerge between members of the Commission on particular questions may be expressed.

The conclusions and recommendations of the Commission resulting from investigations shall be adopted unanimously.

ARTICLE 16

For the exercise of its functions the Commission shall, as necessary, set up inspection teams, on which the three member-States of the Commission shall be equally represented. Each member-State of the Commission shall ensure the presence of its own representatives both on the Commission and on the inspection teams, and shall promptly replace them in the event of their being unable to perform their duties.

It is understood that the dispatch of inspection teams to carry out various specific tasks takes place with the concurrence of the Royal Government of Laos. The points to which the Commission and its inspection teams go for the purposes of investigation and their length of stay at those points shall be determined in relation to the requirements of the particular investigation.

ARTICLE 17

The Commission shall have at its disposal the means of communication and transport required for the performance of its duties. These as a rule will be provided to the Commission by the Royal Government of Laos for payment on mutually acceptable terms, and those which the Royal Government of Laos cannot provide will be acquired by the Commission from other sources. It is understood that the means of communication and transport will be under the administrative control of the Commission.

ARTICLE 18

The costs of the operations of the Commission shall be borne by the members of the Conference in accordance with the provisions of this Article.

(a) The Governments of Canada, India and Poland shall pay the personal salaries and allowances of their nationals who are members of their delegations to the Commission and its subsidiary organs.

(b) The primary responsibility for the provision of accommodation for the Commission and its subsidiary organs shall rest with the Royal Government of Laos, which shall also provide such other local services as may be appropriate. The Commission shall charge to the Fund referred to in sub-paragraph (c) below any local expenses not borne by the Royal Government of Laos.

(c) All other capital or running expenses incurred by

the Commission in the exercise of its functions shall be met from a Fund to which all the members of the Conference shall contribute in the following proportions:

The Governments of the People's Republic of China, France, the Union of Soviet Socialist Republics, the United Kingdom and the United States of America shall contribute 17.6 per cent each.

The Governments of Burma, Cambodia, the Democratic Republic of Viet-Nam, Laos, the Republic of Viet-Nam and Thailand shall contribute 1.5 per cent each.

The Governments of Canada, India and Poland as members of the Commission shall contribute 1 per cent each.

ARTICLE 19

The Co-Chairmen shall at any time, if the Royal Government of Laos so requests, and in any case not later than three years after the entry into force of this Protocol, present a report with appropriate recommendations on the question of the termination of the Commission to the members of the Conference for their consideration. Before making such a report the Co-Chairmen shall hold consultations with the Royal Government of Laos and the Commission.

ARTICLE 20

This Protocol shall enter into force on signature.

It shall be deposited in the archives of the Governments of the United Kingdom and the Union of Soviet Socialist Republics, which shall furnish certified copies thereof to the other signatory States and to all other States of the world.

In witness whereof, the undersigned Plenipotentiaries have signed this Protocol.

Done in two copies in Geneva this twenty-third day of July one thousand and nine hundred and sixty-two in the English, Chinese, French, Laotian and Russian languages, each text being equally authoritative.

FRENCH PROTOCOL ON CONTROL

Presented to the International Conference on the Settlement of the Laotian Question, by Jean Chauvel, on June 6, 1961.

The Governments of ....

    Taking note of the Cease-Fire Agreement signed on ....

    Taking note also of the Statements of .... signed on .... on the Neutrality of Laos, and ....

    Desiring to supplement the Agreement of 20 July 1954 on the Cessation of Hostilities in Laos by provisions designed to ensure that Laotian neutrality will be effectively protected,

Have agreed as follows:

Article 1. The International Commission for Supervision and Control established by Article 25 of the 1954 Agreement shall be responsible for supervision and control of the application of the provisions of the Cease-Fire Agreement signed on ...., the Declarations on the Neutrality of Laos signed on .... and

....

In performing the duties specified in the present Protocol, the Commission shall act in close cooperation with the Government of Laos.

The Government of Laos shall assist the Commission. It shall insure that the assistance requested by the Commission and its services is provided at all administrative and military levels.

Article 2. The Commission shall set up fixed and mobile inspection teams on which the three member States shall be equally represented. The absence of the representative of one of these States shall not prevent the

Commission or any of its teams from performing their functions.

The Commission shall establish for its inspection teams a sufficient number of operation centres to permit efficient operation of the inspection system. These centres shall be set up, in particular, at the main points of entry into and exit from the territory.

The Commission may change its centres if need arises.

Article 3. The Commission and its teams shall have all the authority for investigation, inspection and verification necessary for the performance of their duties, including authority to hear witnesses.

To this end they shall, as of right, have free and unrestricted access by land, sea or air to all parts of Laos, and shall have freedom to inspect, at any time, all aerodromes, installations, or establishments and all units, organizations and activities which are or might be of a military nature.

The Commission and its inspection teams shall have access to aircraft and shipping registers, to manifests and other relevant documents relating to all types of aircraft, vehicles and river craft, whether civil or military, domestic or foreign, and shall have the right to check cargoes and passenger lists.

Article 4. The Commission shall have sufficient logistic resources, including all means of transport and communication required for the effective performance of its duties.

The Commission shall have free use of these means of transport and communication and of the facilities necessary for their maintenance.

Article 5. The Government of Laos shall take all the necessary measures to ensure the safety of the Commission and its inspection teams and, in particular:

(1) it shall grant them full and complete protection including, at their request, the placing of protective forces at their disposal;

(2) it shall take suitable measures to enable them to travel quickly and safely so that they may perform their duties more effectively;

(3) it shall grant them all the privileges and immunities required for the performance of their duties.

Article 6. At the request of the Laotian Government or one of the members of the Commission, the Commission shall investigate without delay any infringement or threatened infringement of the provisions the application of which is subject to its control. Investigations may also be carried out by an inspection team at the request of one of its members.

Article 7. Decisions relating to the operations of the Commission or the inspection teams, and all procedural decisions, shall be taken by majority vote.

Article 8. The inspection teams shall report regularly to the Commission on their work. In addition, they shall immediately report any facts which necessitate urgent measures.

The Commission shall send members of the Conference a quarterly report on its work. In case of urgency, it shall send them special reports and suggest the measures it considers appropriate.

In all cases in which the Commission or one of its teams fail to agree on their reports, they shall submit a majority report and a minority report or three separate reports.

Article 9. The Commission shall remain in being until it is agreed by the members of the Conference that it can be terminated, and in any case until 31 July 1964. The Co-Chairmen shall report to the members of the Confer-

187

ence by that date on the question of continuing the Commission's work.

The Government of Laos or the Commission may at any time propose to members of the Conference the arrangements they consider necessary for adapting the activities and resources of the Commission to the needs of the situation.

Article 10. As long as the Commission remains in being, the heads of the diplomatic missions accredited by the States members of the Conference to the Government of .... shall meet to take note of and discuss the reports of the Commission, which shall be transmitted to them direct. They shall also discuss the proposals and reports provided for in the preceding article. These meetings shall take place at least twice a year and, in case of need, at the request of one of the heads of mission, provided that the majority of the members agree.

Article 11. The expenses of the Commission and its services shall be borne by the members of the Conference as follows: ....

Article 12. The present Protocol replaces the provisions of articles 26 to 40 inclusive of Chapter VI of the 1954 Agreements.

TEN DRAFT ARTICLES TO SUPPLEMENT
THE FRENCH PROTOCOL ON CONTROL

Presented to the International Conference on the Settlement of the Laotian Question, by W. Averell Harriman, on June 20, 1961.

1. The International Control Commission would establish a certain number of inspection posts through which all military personnel or war equipment entering or leaving Laos must pass.

2. The Commission would inform the Laotian Government and the members of the Conference of the installation of these posts.

3. The Laotian factions would inform the Commission of the exact positions of their forces and of the foreign forces cooperating with them.

4. All foreign military personnel or advisers other than those authorised by the 1954 Geneva Agreements would be withdrawn from Laos within a certain period.

5. The Commission will report to the Laotian Government and to the Conference participants on the presence of all armaments or war material in excess of that required by the national Laotian forces, and will suggest where the armaments should be sent.

6. No armaments or war material other than that specified by the Laotian Government in its statement on the organization of its national army will be introduced into Laos.

7. All prisoners-of-war and civilian detainees will be freed within 10 days at most after the entry into effect of the Protocol. The repatriation of those of foreign nationality will be ensured by the Commission.

189

8. There will be neither reprisals nor discrimination against any person or organization due to their activities during the hostilities in Laos.

9. Articles of this Protocol supersede corresponding articles of the 1954 Agreements.

10. The present Protocol will take effect the day it is signed.

DRAFT OUTLINE OF A MODEL TREATY OF NEUTRALIZATION

The Governments of [guarantor states] and the Government of [neutralized state], desiring to establish a status of permanent neutrality for [neutralized state] in the interest of the maintenance of international order and the peaceful development of the peoples concerned, have agreed as follows,

The Government of [neutralized state],

Being resolved to pursue a policy of permanent neutrality,

Solemnly proclaims that,

(1) It will not enter into any alliance or collective security agreements, or participate in any undertaking designed to influence the internal affairs of other countries;

(2) It will not permit the use of its territory by any foreign country for the purpose of establishing military bases or of engaging in activities designed to interfere in the internal affairs of other countries; and will require the withdrawal of such bases and the cessation of such activities as may exist at the time of this declaration;

(3) It will not permit the introduction into its territory of armaments, munitions, and war materials generally, except such quantities of conventional armaments

EXPLANATORY NOTE: This draft outline of a model treaty is intended to illustrate typical attributes of a neutralization regime. As we have stressed repeatedly throughout the text, the concrete embodiment of neutralization depends upon the specific circumstances of particular cases. No single treaty model can hope to provide more than a point of departure. At the same time, assessment of a model treaty does help turn the conception of neutralization into something more tangible than a vague abstraction.

as are necessary for its own internal security and defensive purposes;

(4) It will defend its independence and territorial integrity against interference or attack by any foreign country.[1]

The Governments of [guarantor states],

Being resolved that the independence and permanent neutrality of [neutralized state] will contribute to the maintenance of the international order,

Solemnly declare that,

(1) They recognize and will respect and observe in every way the independence, territorial integrity, and permanent neutrality of [neutralized state];

(2) They will not commit or participate in any act which might directly or indirectly impair the permanent neutrality of [neutralized state], or resort to the use of force or threat of force or any other measure which might impair the peace of [neutralized state];

(3) They will refrain from all direct or indirect interference in the internal affairs of [neutralized state], and will not attach conditions of a political nature to any assistance which they may offer or which [neutralized state] may seek;

---

[1] An additional provision might be inserted at this point with the following general language: "(5) It will not undertake actions or adopt policies that might at some future time involve it in disputes between other countries or groups of countries."

The purpose of such a provision, essential for restrictive forms of neutralization, is to discourage the adoption of certain policies by the neutralized government that might imperil its permanent neutrality. The considerations underlying the possible inclusion of such a provision are discussed in the text in connection with the Swiss attitude toward permanent neutrality. See pp. 22–24. One should not underestimate the difficulties of negotiating, interpreting, and applying such a provision.

(4) They will not bring [neutralized state] in any way into any military alliance or other agreement, whether military or otherwise, which is inconsistent with its neutrality, nor invite or encourage it to enter into any such alliance or to conclude any such agreement;

(5) They will defend the independence and territorial integrity of [neutralized state] and reserve the right to come to its defense separately in the event that joint action cannot be agreed upon;

(6) They will respect the wish of [neutralized state] not to recognize the protection of any alliance or military coalition;

(7) They will not introduce into [neutralized state] foreign troops or military personnel in any form whatsoever, nor will they in any way facilitate or condone the introduction of any foreign troops or military personnel;

(8) They will not establish nor will they in any way facilitate or connive at the establishment in [neutralized state] of any foreign military base, foreign strong point, or other foreign military installation of any kind;

(9) They will not use the territory of [neutralized state] for interference in the internal affairs of other countries;

(10) They will not use the territory of any country, including their own, for interference in the internal affairs of [neutralized state].

The Governments of [guarantor states] and the Government of [neutralized state],

Being resolved to work jointly to establish and maintain the status of permanent neutrality as an important international institution,

Solemnly proclaim that,

193

(1) They appeal to all other states to recognize, respect, and observe in every way the independence, territorial integrity, and permanent neutrality of [neutralized state] and to refrain from any action inconsistent with these principles or with other provisions of the present treaty;

(2) They will undertake, in the event of a violation or threat of violation of the independence, territorial integrity, or permanent neutrality of [neutralized state], to consult jointly among themselves in order to consider measures which might prove to be necessary to ensure the observance of these principles and the other provisions of the present treaty;

(3) They will establish an International Commission which shall investigate cases where there may be any reasonable grounds for considering that a violation of the provisions of this treaty has occurred;

(4) They will provide the International Commission with all the resources and authority necessary for the effective performance of its duties, including fixed and mobile inspection teams, in sufficient number, with adequate access to transportation and communications, and equipped with the necessary legal documents;

(5) They will recommend to the other members of the United Nations, with a view to safeguarding the status of member states undertaking a policy of permanent neutrality, that the Charter be revised to the end that permanently neutral states: will not be candidates for membership in the Security Council, will not be called upon to participate in military, economic, or political sanctions against other states, and will be permitted to absent themselves from voting in the General Assembly on issues in regard to which an expression of

opinion might at some future time involve them in disputes between other countries or groups of countries;

(6) They will consult as necessary to review the provisions of this treaty, on the understanding that no changes will be made in its provisions without the concurrence of [guarantor states] and [neutralized state];

(7) They will agree to convene a meeting of representatives of [guarantor states] and [neutralized state] within six months of receiving a request for such a meeting from any signatory of the treaty.

OTHER BOOKS PUBLISHED FOR
THE CENTER OF INTERNATIONAL STUDIES
PRINCETON UNIVERSITY

Gabriel A. Almond, *The Appeals of Communism*

Gabriel A. Almond and James S. Coleman, editors, *The Politics of the Developing Areas*

Gabriel A. Almond and Sidney Verba, *The Civic Culture: Political Attitudes and Democracy in Five Nations*

Richard J. Barnet and Richard A. Falk, editors, *Security in Disarmament*

Henry Bienen, *Tanzania: Party Transformation and Economic Development*

Cyril E. Black and Thomas P. Thornton, editors, *Communism and Revolution: The Strategic Uses of Political Violence*

Cyril E. Black, Richard A. Falk, Klaus Knorr, Oran R. Young, *Neutralization and World Politics*

Robert J. C. Butow, *Tojo and the Coming of the War*

Miriam Camps, *Britain and the European Community, 1955–1963*

Bernard C. Cohen, *The Political Process and Foreign Policy: The Making of the Japanese Peace Settlement*

Bernard C. Cohen, *The Press and Foreign Policy*

Charles De Visscher, *Theory and Reality in Public International Law*, translated by P. E. Corbett

Frederick S. Dunn, *Peace-making and the Settlement with Japan*

Harry Eckstein, *Division and Cohesion in Democracy: A Study of Norway*

Richard A. Falk, *Legal Order in a Violent World*

Robert Gilpin, *France in the Age of the Scientific State*

Richard F. Hamilton, *Affluence and the French Worker in the Fourth Republic*

Herman Kahn, *On Thermonuclear War*

W. W. Kaufmann, editor, *Military Policy and National Security*

Klaus Knorr, *On the Uses of Military Power in the Nuclear Age*

Klaus Knorr, *The War Potential of Nations*

Klaus Knorr, editor, *NATO and American Security*

Klaus Knorr and James N. Rosenau, editors, *Contending Approaches to International Politics*

Klaus Knorr and Sidney Verba, editors, *The International System: Theoretical Essays*